"Unlike many devotional books that give you all the answers, Sally's book will encourage you in your walk with God. Each day is an invitation to spend time with Jesus. Not only will you find love letters from him, but there is plenty of room for you to write your thoughts and prayers back to him. Let this coming year be the year you spend time with your best friend, Jesus."

—SAMANTHA LANDY, host, Psalms of Hope radio program

"People who help us ponder the wonder of the character of our God are a marvelous gift to God's people. Sally Auguston has done just that in *Meet My God*. She will lead you through daily devotionals . . . to a deepened worship of the Lord of glory. Take and read and marvel."

—GERRY BRESHEARS, Professor of Theology, Western Seminary

"Whether as a new believer or seasoned saint, *Meet My God* promises to capture your heart and deepen your conviction that the infinite lover of our souls is intimate yet majestic, personal yet worthy of worship, all-loving yet transforming. Sally's compelling choice of Scriptures . . . is equally matched by her simple but honest, heartfelt prayers. Expect to be captured as well as cherished as you daily open your heart to our infinite yet intimate God."

—PHYLLIS BENNETT, Director, Women's
Center for Ministry, Western Seminary

"From the very first page, I could feel my soul exhale and reorient toward God. The beauty of this book is simple yet profound—it's actually *about God*. Sally has masterfully crafted a guide that's both theologically rich *and* delightful to read. Give your soul the gift of journeying through this book and rediscover how great our God truly is."

—KARI PATTERSON, author of *Sacred Mundane:
How to Find Freedom, Purpose, and Joy*

"Sally Auguston shares fresh insights on God's person and character, shows the evidence in Scripture, then reflects the impact on her own life in a prayer. These insightful encounters will deepen and enrich your walk with our glorious God who invites us to know him."

—JON DRURY, author of *Lord I Feel So Small*

"I wholeheartedly commend this tremendous collection of devotions. Sally Auguston writes from years of experience loving God, following God, and faithfully serving his church. With a helpful balance of Scripture, meditation, and prayer, she invites us into a deeper experience of knowing the God of Scripture. Wonderful!"

—ADAM McMURRAY, Senior Pastor, River West Church

"Sally Auguston's book is entering the world for 'such a time as this.' This book has the power to help Christians build a renewed intimacy with the living God based on the never-changing Scriptures, not the wavering opinions of the world. *Meet My God* is for new worshipers of God and for those who have walked closely for the long haul: it's a practical reminder of his wonders, his nature, and his depth of love. Take a deep breath as you read this daily devotional, letting its simplicity unravel the complexities of your soul."

—PAMELA HAVEY LAU, author of *A Friend in Me*

"*Meet My God* gives an excellent picture of who God is. I appreciate how Sally authenticates each attribute with Scripture. A plus is that her daily entries include a prayer and a question to ponder. Each devotional is short and rich with thoughts. I enjoy the brevity of each daily reading so I can contemplate her words and Bible passages. This book is like frosting on the cake for daily reading and quiet time."

—SHIRLEY QUIRING MOZENA, author, speaker, and blogger

Meet My God

Meet My God

366 Meditations, Bible Verses, and Prayers
to Help You Know God More Deeply

SALLY SJORDAL AUGUSTON

RESOURCE *Publications* · Eugene, Oregon

MEET MY GOD
366 Meditations, Bible Verses, and Prayers to Help You Know God More Deeply

Copyright © 2021 Sally Sjordal Auguston. All rights reserved. Except for brief quotations in critical publications or reviews, no part of this book may be reproduced in any manner without prior written permission from the publisher. Write: Permissions, Wipf and Stock Publishers, 199 W. 8th Ave., Suite 3, Eugene, OR 97401.

Resource Publications
An Imprint of Wipf and Stock Publishers
199 W. 8th Ave., Suite 3
Eugene, OR 97401

www.wipfandstock.com

PAPERBACK ISBN: 978-1-6667-1255-1
HARDCOVER ISBN: 978-1-6667-1256-8
EBOOK ISBN: 978-1-6667-1257-5

09/13/21

To Bob,
thank you for your love, generosity, patience, prayers, and
encouragement.
You are God's special gift to me.

And to my children and my grandchildren,
I pray that each of you may draw closer to God
and experience the joy of
a very special relationship with him.

We can begin to understand God as we become more knowledgeable through his written word and his Holy Spirit. God has revealed himself, his character, and his nature by word and spiritual revelation. He beckons us to come to him and to know him.

— AllAboutGOD.com

Permissions

Unless otherwise noted, all scriptures are from THE HOLY BIBLE, NEW
INTERNATIONAL VERSION®. Copyright © 1973, 1978, 1984, 2011 by Biblica,
Inc.™. Used by permission of Zondervan.

American King James Version (AKJV) Scripture quotations marked (AKJV) are taken
from the AMERICAN KING JAMES VERSION, 1899, public domain.

Amplified Bible, Classic Edition (AMPCE) Scripture quotation marked (AMPCE) is
taken from the Amplified Bible, Copyright © 1954, 1958, 1962, 1964, 1965, 1987
by The Lockman Foundation. Used by permission.

Aramaic Bible in Plain English (ABPE) Scripture quotation marked (ABPE) is taken
from the ARAMAIC BIBLE IN PLAIN ENGLISH, 2010 copyright ©, Rev. David
Bauscher, Lulu Enterprises Incorporated, 2010.

Bible in Basic English (BBE) Scripture quotations marked (BBE) are taken from the
1949/1964 BIBLE IN BASIC ENGLISH, public domain.

Complete Jewish Bible (CJB) Scripture quotation marked (CJB) is taken from the
COMPLETE JEWISH BIBLE, copyright © 1998 by David H. Stern. Published by
Jewish New Testament Publications, Inc. www.messianicjewish.net. Distributed
by Messianic Jewish Resources Int'l. www.messianicjewish.net. All rights
reserved. Used by permission.

Douay-Rheims Bible (DRB) Scripture quotations marked (DRB) are taken from the
1899 DOUAY-RHEIMS BIBLE, public domain.

English Revised Version (ERV) Scripture quotations marked (ERV) are taken from
the ENGLISH REVISED VERSION, 1885, public domain.

English Standard Version (ESV) Scripture quotations marked (ESV) are taken from
THE HOLY BIBLE, ENGLISH STANDARD VERSION®, copyright © 2001 by
Crossway, a publishing ministry of Good News Publishers. Used by permission.

Holman Christian Standard Bible (HCSB) Scripture quotations marked (HCSB) are
taken from the HOLMAN CHRISTIAN STANDARD BIBLE, copyright © 1999,
2000, 2002, 2003 by Holman Bible Publishers, Nashville Tennessee. All rights
reserved.

International Standard Version (ISV) Scripture quotations marked (ISV) are taken
from the INTERNATIONAL STANDARD VERSION, copyright © 1996–2008
by the ISV Foundation. All rights reserved internationally.

Jubilee Bible 2000 (JUB) Scripture quotation marked (JUB) is taken from the Jubilee
Bible, copyright © 2000, 2001, 2010, 2013 by Life Sentence Publishing, Inc. Used

Content in digital sites BibleHub.com, BibleGateway.com, Bible.com, BibleStudyTools.com were helpful in aligning the word or phrase of the day with Scripture verses.

The epigraph was sourced from "Infinite God." All About GOD Ministries, AllAboutGOD.com. https://www.allaboutgod.com/infinite-god.htm.

The poem, "Finding Him," was crafted for this devotional, copyright © 2021 by Lynn Champagne.

Note: In some Scripture references, words in brackets were added by the author to provide context.

Acknowledgments

I owe a tremendous debt of gratitude to:

The Holy Spirit for his inspiration and for carrying me throughout this project.

Donna Scales, creator of "My Dictionary of Praise," a booklet with a page for each letter of the alphabet with "starter" words describing who God is and what he does. That booklet was this project's spark.

Mary Ann Noack, Women's Pastor at River West Church in Lake Oswego, Oregon, who recognized my daily written meditation on a word per day for what it was, a devotional-to-be.

My mom, Mel Sjordal, and my sister, Bonnie Adkins, who avidly read first and second drafts of this book and provided on-target input as well as encouragement and prayers.

My dad, Bob Sjordal, for his quiet confidence in my ability, with God's help, to get 'er done.

Lynn Champagne, who prayed throughout the development of this book. She contributed wise and loving advice at critical junctures and crafted the inspirational poem, "Finding Him," on the following page.

The women in my small groups in The River Women's Bible Study and to the Wednesday Noon Prayer group, whose prayers upheld me throughout this project.

The people in our River West Church home group, for their affirmation and faithful prayer support.

And, thank you for purchasing *Meet My God*. All net income from the sale of this book will be donated to advance God's work in our world. May his harvest be plentiful.

Finding Him

I scurry around.
Running late. Again.
Heart racing.
Thoughts jumbled.
I am lost in my scramble,
out of breath, when
His voice beckons,

Be still, and know
that I am God.
It calms me,
reminds me I am His
and He is mine.
In the warmth of His cloak,
He enfolds me.

The Lord is my Shepherd.
When I am lost,
He finds me.
His sturdy arms
carry me home,
cradled in the promise
I'll never be alone.

He is my Father,
giving me His Spirit;
my Deliverer,
lavishing me with grace;
my Creator who knows me
fully, yet draws near
in unconditional love.

I pause, take deep,
unhurried breaths,
open my Bible,
and feel His quiet peace
wash over me.
In the Word, I find Him.
In Him, I find Me.

—Lynn Champagne

Introduction

This devotional book invites you to better understand who my God is, what he is like, and what he does. My God is the God of the Bible. In that amazing book, he has revealed so much about himself. While we can never fully comprehend who God is and what he is like, he is calling us to explore the Bible, to discover more about him, and to draw near to him. Using relatable terms, *Meet My God* features a word or phrase for each day of the year, with scriptural proof that God has revealed each of these things about himself. By meditating on the word of the day throughout each day, you will open up your mind and heart to experience a deeper understanding of and relationship with God.

Within each month, the words about God are organized into eight categories:

1. The (very) big picture: We begin our exploration *before* the beginning; God has always existed. No one made him. He created everything that ever existed. Everything about him is the ultimate: the ultimate in goodness, in power, in wisdom, in love. While he is too great, too vast, too *everything* to fully know, we first try to get a glimpse of his scope, to bathe in the wonder of him. As we delve into his character and what God is like, we find that the Lord is the best of everything, perfection in every attribute. When we consider what he is like, we can't help being awestruck.

2. The beginning: Shifting gears, we reflect on who he is and what he did during "the beginning." The book of Genesis says, "In the beginning, God created . . ." At this point in Scripture, God as Creator (*Elohim*) is plural. God, Jesus, and the Holy Spirit together have existed from before the beginning of time. Out of timelessness, they created time. Together, they created all things, and being all-knowing, they knew what to do and what would happen. So God set his grand plan into

motion. We pause to think about him giving birth to all that is, including each one of us. Indeed, one of the many names of God is *El Chuwl* (The One Who Gave You Birth).

3. Desiring relationship with us: More than Creator (he did not stop at creation—giving birth to all that is—then just allow things to proceed), God is relational. He loves us and does not consider us insignificant. He created us to be in relationship with him. He is Immanuel (God With Us), Abba (Daddy), and our Confessor who loves us unconditionally. How can we not be awed by the opportunity to be in loving relationship with the Creator of the universe?

4. Nurturing and sustaining us: Next, we ponder the wonderful ways of the Good Shepherd. We observe that he cares for and nurtures us. Because of God's abundant, overflowing love for us, he does everything he can for our wellbeing. He blesses us, giving us strength, wisdom, and encouragement. His watchcare is the only reason we can survive in this world. He sustains and maintains us, providing everything we need for our sustenance. Day in and day out, he is *Jehovah Jireh* (The God Who Provides). When we are injured or ailing, he is *Jehovah Rapha* (The God Who Heals). He does all of this to maintain us according to his plan.

5. Judging us: Having meditated on his character at the beginning of the month, we know that God is righteous. Being perfect and all-wise, he will judge. When he does that, he will, of course, find us sinful. He knows all of our flaws and failings. When we consider his perfect character and exalted position as he judges, we see our desperate need for deliverance.

6. Delivering us: We know that we need someone who is powerful and able to save us, no matter what. That someone is surely God. One of his Hebrew names, *El Gibhor*, means that he is strong, mighty, valiant, heroic. He is the banner under which we march. He fights for us and protects us.

7. Transforming us: Hallelujah! He has rescued us from our lost state, but we know we need—in fact, we earnestly desire—transformation. As we consider all of our failings, the magnitude of the needed change is intimidating, seemingly impossible. But God knows what we need. Being loving, strong, and mighty, God is indeed able to transform us. And when he does begin to transform us, it verifies our testimony. We were lost; now we have been found. We can have confidence that he will make everything right in the end.

8. Anticipating eternity: God is Lord of Hosts (*Lord Sabbaoth*), Lord of everything, and he will accomplish his plan for us. Everything will work out perfectly, of course, because he is in charge. God is everlasting (*El Olam*), outside of time, the beginning and the end. We can look forward to "the finish line" which is an incredibly beautiful eternity with him. Yes, we can have the sure hope of peace forever because we know we will be with him. The Bible tells us how the story ends. He himself is our peace (*Jehovah Shalom*). During the final days of each month, we reflect on who he is and what he does during and following his inevitable great victory.

As we finish each month reflecting on a magnificent eternity in his presence, it's only fitting that we begin the next month by again considering the (very) big picture of who he is.

On each page, the author has included her own prayer relating to that day's word and the associated Scripture verses, providing a view into her own heart as she studied and learned. She has posed questions pertaining to each day's aspect of God with the hope that you will write *your own* reflections. This will help you capture insights that the Holy Spirit is laying on your heart and grow deeper in your relationship with God. The author's dear desire is that in reading about her God's love and gracious involvement in our lives, your understanding of him will be deepened, and your walk with him will be enriched.

Today God is inviting you to learn about him, to experience him more deeply, and to be awestruck by the wonder of him. Answer his invitation; it will be literally life-changing.

God (with a capital G)

When we think about it, there are lots of gods in this world. People admire—practically worship—science, achievement, physical fitness, money, success, youth, creativity, even fashion. But these gods are false, powerless. They pale in comparison with the one God who created and still rules the universe. God (with a capital G) is the source of all moral authority and is the supreme being worshiped by Christians the world around.

> In the beginning God created the heavens and the earth.
> —Genesis 1:1, ESV

> I am the LORD your God, who brought you out of the land of
> Egypt, out of the house of slavery. You shall have no other gods
> before me . . . You shall not bow down to them or serve them.
> —Exodus 20:2–3, 5a, ESV

> And as soon as we heard it, our hearts melted, and there was
> no spirit left in any man because of you, for the LORD your
> God, he is God in the heavens above and on the earth beneath.
> —Joshua 2:11, ESV

My prayer: Lord God, it is right to begin this book by referencing the beginning of the story that you wrote. You created heaven and earth. You created all things. Only you could have planned, made, and filled such a marvelous, intricate, enormous universe; there is none like you. In all things, at all times, please help me to remember who you are and to honor you only.

What have been some of the "little g" gods in your life?

Yahweh/Jehovah

In Judeo-Christian Scripture, this is the most frequently used name for the one true God. The name means Adonai, Master, or Lord. By Jewish tradition, the name of God is too holy, too sacred to be spoken and is written in the ancient Hebrew language without vowels, YHWH (also YHVH, JHVH, or JHWH in English). When vowels were added, the name became "Yahweh," "Yahveh," "Jehovah," or "Jehowah."

> I appeared to Abraham, Isaac, and Jacob as God Almighty, but
> I did not reveal My name Yahweh to them.
> —Exodus 6:3, HCSB

> When all the people saw it [the fire of the LORD that consumed
> the sacrifice], they fell facedown and said, "Yahweh, He is God!
> Yahweh, He is God!" —1 Kings 18:39, HCSB

My prayer: Lord and Master, thank you for introducing yourself and for showing me many of the names that represent your characteristics: Provider, Shepherd, Healer, Banner, Most High. Because I know some of your names, I now feel closer to you as Creator and Sustainer of the entire universe. I do not call upon "the universe" to help me or show me. I call upon the only one who matters, from before time began into eternity.

How do you respond when someone calls upon "the universe" to help them?

I AM WHO I AM

In the Bible, Moses was concerned about how to talk about God to the people in Egypt who worshiped many gods. God's explanation of himself was, "I AM WHO I AM." That may not sound very helpful, but it expresses his vastness. It means that God is the only being who is self-existent, with no source. He is eternally present with no past, no future, no time, no space, no beginning, and no end.

> God said to Moses, "I AM WHO I AM." And he said, "Say this to the people of Israel: 'I AM has sent me to you.'" —Exodus 3:14, ESV

> For I am the LORD, your God, the Holy One of Israel, your Savior. —Isaiah 43:3, ESV

> Listen to me, O Jacob, and Israel, whom I called: I am he [the Lord]; I am the first and I am the last. My hand laid the foundation of the earth, and my right hand spread out the heavens; when I call to them, they stand forth together.
> —Isaiah 48:12–13, ESV

My prayer: Yahweh, that you have always existed, and never not existed, is impossible to wrap my mind around. Yet I can grasp that you had to exist before creation. I know that you are here now and have never left. You inhabit the future, holding all of time in your hands. You are the Lord; there is none like you.

How can a person wrap their mind around a being so vast and mysterious?

Holy/pure

To be holy is to be so pure as to be set apart, to be "other than" everyone and everything in this universe. God is so pure, so perfect in goodness that he is different from every created thing. He wants us to be holy—pure and set apart—as well; he has made a way for us to be cleansed from our impurity, our sin, so that we can be in his presence.

> But like the Holy One who called you, be holy yourselves also in all your behavior; because it is written: "You shall be holy, for I am holy." —1 Peter 1:15–16, NASB 2020

> And the four living creatures, each of them with six wings, are full of eyes all around and within, and day and night they never cease to say, "Holy, holy, holy, is the Lord God Almighty, who was and is and is to come!" —Revelation 4:8, ESV

My prayer: Lord, in my quest to know you, I confess that I often neglect to acknowledge your holiness. I just boldly come near. You are holy, holy, holy, and yet you have called me to yourself, adopting me as an heir to your kingdom. May I never be cavalier about you, about knowing you, about your approachability, or about how extraordinary it is to be in relationship with you.

How can we approach God if he is so holy and pure, so set apart from us?

Infinite/unlimited

The human mind cannot comprehend infinity, true limitlessness, but we can describe God as "infinite" or "unlimited" because there is no restriction on him, no boundary, no end to his extent. There is also no limit to his love, kindness, knowledge, wisdom, or power. He is beyond ultimate because there is no end to him.

> Great is our Lord and mighty in power; his understanding has no limit. —Psalm 147:5

> Ah, Sovereign LORD, you have made the heavens and the earth by your great power and outstretched arm. Nothing is too hard for you. —Jeremiah 32:17

> For the one whom God has sent speaks the words of God, for God gives the Spirit without limit. —John 3:34

My prayer: Sovereign Lord, your word tells me that your goodness, wisdom, power, love, and understanding have no limit. I know that you are pouring into my cup so that it overflows with the blessings and forgiveness that can only come from you, the limitless one, who was, and is, and is to come. I praise you for all of this that is far beyond my understanding.

What aspects of God's limitlessness are most important to you?

Creator

The proper noun, Creator, used as a name for God, recognizes that he is the one who brought everything into existence, the only one who could have accomplished it all. Everything from nothing, the vast reaches of space to the intricacies of subatomic particles, and all of their interdependencies, he perfectly created it all.

> I am the LORD, your Holy One, the Creator of Israel, your King. —Isaiah 43:15, ESV

> Have you not known? Have you not heard? The LORD is the everlasting God, the Creator of the ends of the earth. He does not faint or grow weary; his understanding is unsearchable. —Isaiah 40:28, ESV

> For you created my inmost being; you knit me together in my mother's womb. —Psalm 139:13

My prayer: Lord, I know that you created all things because your word says so. Many of the most intelligent scientists—people who are taught to question everything—are even brought to the realization that only you could have done this. Creation did not just happen. Everything in all of creation is so deeply and intricately designed. All of it fits together so beautifully, so perfectly. Thank you for creating me to love and serve you and for enabling me to see and appreciate your wondrous works.

How do you think it would feel to be plopped right into the original garden of Eden?

Light

Light is a metaphor for truth. God embodies all truth; he is the opposite of darkness. When we celebrate God, referring to him as *Light*, we acknowledge his power over darkness. Darkness and light cannot coexist. Light will always dispel darkness; darkness cannot overcome light. On the first day of creation, God created light and saw that it was good, and thus, he could continue his good work.

> The LORD is my light and my salvation; whom shall I fear? The
> LORD is the stronghold of my life; of whom shall I be afraid?
> —Psalm 27:1, ESV

> This is the message we have heard from him and proclaim to
> you, that God is light, and in him is no darkness at all.
> —1 John 1:5, ESV

> The people who walked in darkness have seen a great light;
> those who dwelt in a land of deep darkness, on them has light
> shone. —Isaiah 9:2, ESV

My prayer: Lord, your light, your truth, is powerful because it leads to salvation. And your light is beautiful, even though it discloses the ugliness of sin. Your light is an invitation out of darkness, guiding the way onto the path of righteousness. Thank you for bringing me out of darkness and into your perfect light.

For you, when did the light at the end of the tunnel become the way out of darkness?

Author

We can think of God not only as Creator, but also as Author. He wrote the story of our existence. He knew we would be enticed by and overcome by sin, and as a result we could not be in his holy presence. The description of God as the "Author of eternal salvation" recognizes that he provided the end of our story, when we will be saved from eternal separation from him.

> Your eyes saw my unformed body; all the days ordained for me were written in your book before one of them came to be. —Psalm 139:16

> And being made perfect, he became the author of eternal salvation unto all them that obey him. —Hebrews 5:9, KJV

> But nothing unclean will ever enter it [the Holy City], nor anyone who does what is detestable or false, but only those who are written in the Lamb's book of life —Revelation 21:27, ESV

My prayer: Lord, you wrote the story of humankind, and you wrote my story. You know the beginning, middle, and the end of all things, including my own. Thank you for guiding me through each chapter of my life and for authoring a perfect ending for me in eternity with you.

How have you felt God's hand in writing the latest chapter in your life?

Breathes

Breathing—the respiration process—is divided into inspiration (inhalation) and expiration (exhalation). *Inspired* ideas may have been breathed into a person by God. Yes, God does that: he breathes into us to give us life, direction, even ideas. We need him as much as we need each breath.

> Then the LORD God formed a man from the dust of the ground and breathed into his nostrils the breath of life, and the man became a living being. —Genesis 2:7

> But after the three and a half days the breath of life from God entered them, and they stood on their feet, and terror struck those who saw them. —Revelation 11:11

My prayer: Lord God, you are my life force, my breath of life. You breathed into me from my beginning, and you sustain me. My original breath was a particular miracle, the one that gave me life outside my mother's womb. Even more miraculous was the breath of my rebirth, as your Holy Spirit filled my very being, giving me eternal life with you. Day by day, I love to experience your inspiration, ideas that, when acted upon, will please and glorify you.

In what way has God inspired (breathed into) you in recent times?

Active

God did not create the world and then just sit back, starting with his first day of rest, saying, "Well, that work is done." He continued to be involved. And even now, he doesn't just watch things unfold; he engages with our lives. He takes action, either behind the scenes or in the midst of the battle.

> Behold, God does all these things [delivering him], twice, three times, with a man, to bring back his soul from the pit, that he may be lighted with the light of life —Job 33:29–30, ESV

> For the LORD your God is the one who goes with you to fight for you against your enemies to give you victory.
> —Deuteronomy 20:4

> For it is God who works in you to will and to act in order to fulfill his good purpose. —Philippians 2:13

My prayer: Lord, history is rich with examples of your involvement. Even now in modern times, you continue to be active. You have delivered me time and again from mortal danger. While I wait for answers to my prayers, I can be confident that I am not enduring a gap of nothingness; you are acting, putting the pieces into place. What's more, I know that you are actively working in me to transform me into the person you want me to be. Thank you for having a plan for my life and for continuing to act to fulfill your good plan.

How does it help you to know that God is actively working in your life, either behind the scenes or in the midst of the battle?

Father

God has the position and authority as the head of the family of humankind. As head of the family, he provides for everyone and everything in all of his creation. He seeks the best for each of us and wants us to have a true feeling of unity and love toward one another.

> For you are our Father, though Abraham does not know us, and Israel does not acknowledge us; you, O LORD, are our Father, our Redeemer from of old is your name. —Isaiah 63:16, ESV

> [Jesus said,] "Pray then like this: 'Our Father in heaven, hallowed be your name.'" —Matthew 6:9, ESV

> Jesus said to her, "Do not cling to me, for I have not yet ascended to the Father; but go to my brothers and say to them, 'I am ascending to my Father and your Father, to my God and your God.'" —John 20:17, ESV

My prayer: Father, I am so glad that you adopted me to be one of your children. Your word says it is now my right to call you Father. I cherish the unbreakable bond I have with you. You are a good and loving Father who provides for all of my needs. Thank you for hearing my praises, for caring about my concerns, and for carrying my burdens.

In what ways has God been a good father to you?

Immanuel

When Jesus' mother Mary became pregnant, the angel told her that her son would be called Immanuel. Not a first name, this is a masculine personal title that comes from the Hebrew *Immanu'el*, which literally means "God is with us." God had chosen to come to earth to dwell with us. And he is with us now.

> Devise your strategy, but it will be thwarted; propose your plan, but it will not stand, for God is with us. —Isaiah 8:10
>
> "I am with you," declares the LORD. —Haggai 1:13b
>
> "Behold, the virgin shall conceive and bear a son, and they shall call his name Immanuel" (which means, God with us). —Matthew 1:23, ESV

My prayer: Lord, you have been with people since our beginning, and you chose to live a life on earth to exhibit your wisdom and love through the person of Jesus. In doing so, you made a way for us to spend eternity with you. Because I know and love you, I have confidence that you are with me at all times with your good and perfect plan for me. There is nothing for me to fear.

How does it feel to know that God is literally with you at all times?

Responds/answers

God participates in relationship with us by listening to what we have to say and responding. Because he cares, he answers us through actions or sometimes through what seems like inaction. (Yes, silence can be a response. It doesn't mean he is not listening.) Sometimes we ask, but don't wait for his response, or we don't listen to the response when it comes. Sometimes we don't even ask for his direction, and that is regrettable because he always has our best interests in mind.

> I call upon you, for you will answer me, O God; incline your ear to me; hear my words. —Psalm 17:6, ESV

> When he calls to me, I will answer him; I will be with him in trouble; I will rescue him and honor him. —Psalm 91:15, ESV

> Delight yourself in the LORD, and he will give you the desires of your heart. —Psalm 37:4, ESV

My prayer: Loving Lord, you are ever near. We are in an ever-deepening relationship. Because you know my heart, you know that I am not in a relationship with you in order to get something I want. Still, because we are in relationship, I know you hear me, and when I ask anything, you respond by showing me or providing exactly what I need—which might not be what I have asked for. Thank you for hearing my true heart's desire, for knowing what I really need, and for responding in the best possible way.

One aspect of a loving relationship is that we respond to each other. In what ways does God respond to you?

Shepherd

One of God's Hebrew names is *Jehovah Rajah,* which means The Lord My Shepherd. As our shepherd, God guides or directs us on the best path. He protects us physically and spiritually from our enemies, and he provides everything we need.

> The LORD is my shepherd; I shall not want. —Psalm 23:1, ESV
>
> I am the good shepherd. The good shepherd lays down his life for the sheep. —John 10:11, ESV
>
> For you were straying like sheep, but have now returned to the Shepherd and Overseer of your souls. —1 Peter 2:25, ESV

My prayer: Lord, you are the Good Shepherd; how extensively you care for me in every way! You guide, feed, anoint, rescue; the list goes on. Thank you for being my personal shepherd. Thank you for knowing me, watching over me, and leading me in the right direction.

As your personal shepherd, how has God taken care of you?

Beneficent

God's nature is to act in ways that are kind, charitable, generous, beneficial, and philanthropic (literally *love of humanity*). God deploys his magnificent power to nurture and sustain us, continually demonstrating his goodwill for us.

> In him we have redemption through his blood, the forgiveness of sins, in accordance with the riches of God's grace that he lavished on us. With all wisdom and understanding, he made known to us the mystery of his will according to his good pleasure, which he purposed in Christ. —Ephesians 1:7–9

> But when the kindness of God our Savior and his love for mankind appeared, he saved us, not on the basis of deeds which we have done in righteousness, but according to his mercy, by the washing of regeneration and renewing by the Holy Spirit, whom he poured out upon us richly through Jesus Christ our Savior. —Titus 3:4–6

My prayer: Kind and loving God, you loved all people, and did you ever give! You gave an unfathomable gift when you gave us your Son. He taught us about you and modeled what love is. I pray that I may more and more show kindness and charity to others so that they may have a glimpse of you. And I pray that if they see something about you in my acts, you will receive the glory.

In responding to others, how do you reflect God's giving nature?

Cares

God is intensely interested in us. He feels concern for us and the choices we make. We are so important to him that at times he comes to rescue us. And because he cares, he looks after us and provides for our needs.

> The LORD is good, a refuge in times of trouble. He cares for those who trust in him. —Nahum 1:7
>
> Are not two sparrows sold for a penny? Yet not one of them will fall to the ground outside your Father's care. And even the very hairs of your head are all numbered. So don't be afraid; you are worth more than many sparrows. —Matthew 10:29–31
>
> Cast all your anxiety on him because he cares for you. —1 Peter 5:7

My prayer: Loving God, your Scriptures detail so many times and ways that you have cared for your people, even long in advance of when the actual events were to occur. The book of my life includes many ways—from big picture to tiniest detail—that you have cared for me physically, emotionally, and spiritually. Because you care for me, you have nurtured the gifts you have given to me; they are everything I need to accomplish your good purpose.

At what time did God show that he cared for you physically, emotionally, or spiritually?

Observes

People want to be noticed, to be seen. It gives us a feeling of significance, that we matter. One of God's Hebrew names, *El Roi,* means The God Who Sees. When God observes us, he notices or perceives whatever is going on in our lives as well as in our hearts, and he registers those things as being important, including all of the details. Because he observes these things, he arrives at a correct judgment.

> So she [Hagar] called the LORD who spoke to her: The God Who Sees, for she said, "In this place, have I actually seen the One who sees me?" —Genesis 16:13, HCSB

> When the LORD looks down from heaven, he observes every human being. —Psalm 33:13, ISV

> The LORD is in his holy temple; the LORD is on his heavenly throne. He observes everyone on earth; his eyes examine them. —Psalm 11:4

My prayer: More than seeing, Lord, you *observe* the significant things, in fact all things, that are going on in my heart. I am so thankful that as you observe my thoughts and deeds, it is with the covering of righteousness provided by your Son, Jesus Christ, my Savior. When judgment time comes, I would surely perish in an instant without that precious cloak.

God sees the real you. What are some of the important things about your heart and life that you would like others to notice?

Perceives

God is perfectly perceptive. He is able to see, hear, feel, and understand what even people who are close to us cannot fully grasp. He senses what is in our hearts and minds, and he understands everything completely. He knows the backdrop as well as what is yet to come. He knows us far better than we can ever know ourselves.

> If you say, "But we knew nothing about this," does not he who weighs the heart perceive it? Does not he who guards your life know it? Will he not repay everyone according to what they have done? —Proverbs 24:12

> You know when I sit and when I rise; you perceive my thoughts from afar. You discern my going out and my lying down; you are familiar with all my ways —Psalm 139:2–3

My prayer: Lord, you are perfect in your knowledge and understanding. You discern exactly what is in my heart and what my motivations are. I praise you for knowing me so thoroughly, and yet loving me and having a plan for me.

What is there about you that God perceives but is hard for regular people to grasp?

Lawgiver

As the prime lawgiver, God has the authority to draw up laws and make them known, which he does through the Bible. He has preserved his laws, statutes, and commandments throughout the ages for our good.

> For the LORD is our judge; the LORD is our lawgiver; the LORD is our king; he will save us. —Isaiah 33:22, ESV

> There is only one lawgiver and judge, he who is able to save and to destroy. But who are you to judge your neighbor? —James 4:12, ESV

My prayer: Righteous God, you gave us your law to help us live in right relationship with you and with each other. Along with everything else you established, your law was perfect. Simplifying your law, to love you with all of my heart, soul, mind, and strength, and my neighbor as myself, provides perfect instruction regarding how to live. But I fail, daily. Thank you for your grace which covers me from my just penalty, so that I can be with you.

Why is it a good thing that God set forth his Law in the Bible?

Challenges

When we are off on a tangent, God lets us know that he objects to our think-ing or behavior and helps us see the truth. He challenges us to put forth special effort and truly do our best, to live our lives for him, and to trust in him even in difficult times.

> Set forth your case, says the LORD; bring your proofs, says the King of Jacob. —Isaiah 41:21, ESV

> And he said to all, "If anyone would come after me, let him deny himself and take up his cross daily and follow me. For whoever would save his life will lose it, but whoever loses his life for my sake will save it. For what does it profit a man if he gains the whole world and loses or forfeits himself?" —Luke 9:23–25, ESV

My prayer: Lord, you do challenge my thinking and my ways. Although it is uncomfortable for me at times, I know that you challenge me for my good. Your best challenge is to believe in, follow, and proclaim the name and the works of your Son, Jesus. Thank you for this and for every good challenge you have for me, now and in the future.

What uncomfortable challenge from God have you recognized as being for your good?

Descends

God inhabits the highest heaven and descends from that high place every time he comes down to help us. His most significant descent was to take the form of a human—Jesus—leaving heaven to live a real human life. He came down to our level to fulfill his promises and to show us how to live.

> And I have come down to deliver them out of the hand of the
> Egyptians and to bring them up out of that land to a good
> and broad land, a land flowing with milk and honey.
> —Exodus 3:8a, ESV

> For I have come down from heaven, not to do my own will but
> the will of him who sent me. —John 6:38, ESV

My prayer: God, it thrills me that you descended from heaven. In Jesus Christ, you left your heavenly place and showed the world how to live, how to relate to one another; you perfectly demonstrated your own character. Thank you for this unspeakably great gift!

We live in a broken world. Why do you think it matters that Jesus left his high place in heaven to live here?

Strong tower

The image of a strong tower is something even better than a watchtower; it is a particularly strong refuge offering extraordinary protection. God is described as a strong tower. When we trust in him, he is an unassailable refuge for us. We can run to him, and he will protect us.

> From the end of the earth I call to you when my heart is faint. Lead me to the rock that is higher than I, for you have been my refuge, a strong tower against the enemy. —Psalm 61:2–3, ESV

> The name of the LORD is a strong tower; the righteous man runs into it and is safe. —Proverbs 18:10, ESV

My prayer: Lord, you are my refuge. I have assurance that I can run to you and be saved. I must not even try to trust in my own "strong tower" which is built of earthly goods and relationships. I know that they will fail. Only you are strong enough to truly protect and sustain me.

When do you need a strong tower to run into? From what do you need to be saved?

Covers

To shelter, shield, or even conceal us, God puts his special covering over us. Psalm 91, a psalm of protection, includes the image of a mother bird covering her baby with her feathers, under her wing. Like that mother bird, God knows what is best for us, and he covers us when we need protection.

> And the LORD said, "Behold, there is a place by me where you shall stand on the rock, and while my glory passes by I will put you in a cleft of the rock, and I will cover you with my hand until I have passed by." —Exodus 33:21–22, ESV

> And of Benjamin he said, The beloved of the LORD shall dwell in safety by him; and the Lord shall cover him all the day long, and he shall dwell between his shoulders.
> —Deuteronomy 33:12, KJ2000

> He will cover you with his feathers, and under his wings you will find refuge; his faithfulness will be your shield and rampart.
> —Psalm 91:4

My prayer: Lord, I know that I can find refuge under your wing, next to your heart. Your great love has covered me; in good times and bad, I have been blessed by your perfect protection. Thank you.

When have you felt that God was covering you to protect you?

Disciplines

Loving parents discipline their children to guide them into right behavior for a better life. God corrects us by punishment, even by causing or allowing us to suffer, in order to help us be more humble or restrained. He wants us to choose holiness.

> Blessed is the man whom you discipline, O LORD, and whom you teach out of your law. —Psalm 94:12, ESV

> For they disciplined us for a short time as it seemed best to them, but he disciplines us for our good, that we may share his holiness. For the moment all discipline seems painful rather than pleasant, but later it yields the peaceful fruit of righteousness to those who have been trained by it.
> —Hebrews 12:10–11, ESV

My prayer: "We're doing this for your own good," my parents said when having to discipline me. And, Lord, you do the same. You discipline me to guide me so that I will choose the right pathways. Thank you for loving me enough to guide me to make choices that move me toward complete transformation, so that Christ may be glorified.

What is an example of God's effective discipline in your life?

Surprises

Some might be surprised that "surprising" is one of the things that God does. Throughout history, God has caused people to feel astonishment or shock. Yes, he surprises us in good ways and in unsettling ways, but always in love.

> Surprise us with love at daybreak; then we'll skip and dance all the day long. —Psalm 90:14, TM

> Oh, look! God's right here helping! God's on my side, Evil is looping back on my enemies. Don't let up! Finish them off! —Psalm 54:4–5, TM

My prayer: Lord, you have worked in surprising, even astonishing, ways. The foremost surprise was your plan for your divine Son to come to earth as a baby, birthed in a humble stable. This King of creation led a humble, earthly life. Then, he was rejected by people, including religious leaders who plotted to kill him. His death, burial, and resurrection were all astonishing. Yes, you have surprised me in so many ways; the greatest of these was the extent to which you have gone to save me from the just punishment for my sins.

How has God surprised you, in a good way or an unsettling way?

Affirms

When a person affirms something, that thing is stated as a fact, asserted strongly and publicly. In the Bible, God affirms many things (e.g., Christ died to save us from the penalty of our sins; God wants us to live an abundant life; he will never leave us nor forsake us, and God has a good plan for each of us.) In all of these statements and others, God affirms his goodness, his holiness, and his love for each one of us.

> So the LORD God of Israel has this to say about the leaders who are ruling over his people: "You have caused my people to be dispersed and driven into exile. You have not taken care of them. So I will punish you for the evil that you have done. I, the LORD, affirm it!" —Jeremiah 23:2, NET

> "I'm going to affirm my great reputation that has been defiled among the nations (that is, that you have defiled in their midst), and those people will learn that I am the LORD," declares the LORD God, "when I affirm my holiness in front of their very eyes." —Ezekiel 36:23

My prayer: Thank you, Lord, for making it clear to me that I am your beloved child. Through many actions, you encouraged me to put my "Yes" in you. You affirmed me, securing me with your pledge that we would enjoy eternity together. What a glorious affirmation that is. In my mind and heart, you have affirmed your great reputation, and in turn, I say "Yes" to you every day!

What makes it difficult for you to affirm "Yes. I'm all in." to God in every way every day?

Transfers

It is dreadful to realize that we have been needlessly oppressed by guilt and shame, living in darkness. But it is good to learn that God is able to transfer us out of that darkness into his marvelous light. We must simply believe and agree to receive this gift, and he is willing to make the miraculous transfer.

> He has delivered us from the domain of darkness and transferred us to the kingdom of his beloved Son.
> —Colossians 1:13, ESV

> But thank God that, although you used to be slaves of sin, you obeyed from the heart that pattern of teaching you were transferred to, and having been liberated from sin, you became enslaved to righteousness. —Romans 6:17–18, HCSB

My prayer: Lord, as you know, because of my father's job requirements, my family was transferred geographically several times during my youth. These times were challenging, but you meant it all for good. As I look back on my life, the best transfer of all has been your moving me from the enslavement of a life of sin and the accusations of Satan to the promise of eternal life with you. I'm so thankful this best-of-all transfer has been accomplished. There's no going back.

What were the barriers to your transfer from darkness into the light of God?

Perfect/flawless

It is impossible for a human to imagine someone without any blemishes, imperfections, mistakes, or shortcomings, someone who has all of the qualities or characteristics required for perfection. But God is that someone. He is flawless, as good as it is possible to be, in every way.

> This God—his way is perfect; the word of the LORD proves true; he is a shield for all those who take refuge in him.
> —2 Samuel 22:31, ESV

> You therefore must be perfect, as your heavenly Father is perfect.
> —Matthew 5:48, ESV

My prayer: Lord, because you are perfect, there is no need for you to change. Because you are unchanging, I can trust in you. But how am I to be perfect as you are perfect? Only through your help. Thank you for helping me as I am being continually renewed and transformed by the work of your Holy Spirit.

In obeying God, we move toward perfection. What shortcomings are being removed from your life as you obey him?

Beautiful

Beauty is something that is aesthetically pleasing to the senses or mind. As we come to know more and more about the Lord's perfection in every attribute, we glimpse his stunning beauty and yearn for more. We long to see him and to experience the depth of his beauty.

> One thing have I asked of the LORD, that will I seek after: that
> I may dwell in the house of the LORD all the days of my life, to
> gaze upon the beauty of the LORD and to inquire in his temple.
> —Psalm 27:4, ESV
>
> Your eyes will behold the king in his beauty; they will see a
> land that stretches afar. —Isaiah 33:17, ESV

My prayer: Lord, I cannot imagine what it will be like in eternity to gaze upon your beauty, your glory. I will not be able to stop praising you, praising you, praising you. This will not be because of your beauty itself, but because of your character, all that you are: the highest of high, the ultimate in goodness and love.

What aspects of God's character are most beautiful to you today?

Treasure

Some people spend their lives looking for treasure, earthly things of great value. Wise men and women seek God. He is the only treasure worthy of the search. And God promises that when we seek him with all our heart, we will find him.

> In that day he will be your sure foundation, providing a rich store of salvation, wisdom, and knowledge. The fear of the LORD will be your treasure. —Isaiah 33:6, NLT

> If you return to the Almighty, you will be restored; If you remove injustice far from your tent, And put your gold in the dust, and the gold of Ophir among the stones of the brooks, Then the Almighty will be your gold and abundant silver to you. —Job 22:23–25, NASB 2020

> Do not store up for yourselves treasures on earth, where moths and vermin destroy, and where thieves break in and steal. But store up for yourselves treasures in heaven . . . For where your treasure is, there your heart will be also. —Matthew 6:19–21

My prayer: Lord, you are my Treasure. You are so dear to me. You are everything I need, my great Sufficiency. You have shown me not to place importance on earthly things. Your promises are what I hold near to my heart, and I praise you for the deep assurance they provide.

What earthly treasures do you hold dear, and in the end why will they not really matter?

Mysterious/incomprehensible/inscrutable

God's infinite nature makes it impossible for us to fully interpret him. He is actually inexplicable. But he invites us to get to know him better and empowers his Holy Spirit to help us do that. While we cannot completely understand him, we do know that he is greater in every way than we can comprehend. It is encouraging and sobering to know that there is no end to his love, power, knowledge, and goodness.

> Can you find out the deep things of God? Can you find out the limit of the Almighty? —Job 11:7, ESV

> The LORD our God has secrets known to no one. We are not accountable for them, but we and our children are accountable forever for all that he has revealed to us, so that we may obey all the terms of these instructions. —Deuteronomy 29:29, NLT

My prayer: Lord, because you are infinite, it is impossible to fully explain you. Indeed, you have gone to great lengths to make yourself known to me, protecting your word through the ages, providing prophets, even taking the form of a man, Jesus. And yet you are so deep, I will never entirely grasp your fullness. The mystery of you draws me ever nearer to your side, and I want to know you better and better. Thank you for continuing to reveal yourself and your marvelous plan for me.

Does it bother you that God is incomprehensible? Why or why not?

Immortal

We cannot fathom living forever, not being subject to death or decay. As time passes, people age, and the things around us begin to break down. But God will live forever, perfect and unchanging. He has always existed and will always be.

> [God] who alone is immortal and who lives in unapproachable light, whom no one has seen or can see. —1 Timothy 6:16a
>
> To the King of the ages, immortal, invisible, the only God, be honor and glory forever and ever. Amen. —1 Timothy 1:17, ESV

My prayer: Father, I sometimes act as though I will live here on earth forever, and yet I see that time is taking its toll on me and on the world around me. I am comforted to know that at just the right time, I will leave this tattered old world and have a new body when I go to my forever-place with you. You are my Lord and Savior, who lives and reigns now, in the forever past, and in the forever future. I praise you for being with me now and for inviting me to be with you for all eternity.

Who was the longest-lived person you have ever known personally, and how did their final years play out?

Transcendent

God is in a class by himself. He is extraordinary in every way. He is so holy, majestic, perfectly good, and so pure that no evil can be in his presence. No one can lay hold of him. He is infinitely exalted above all creation.

> "Do you people think that I am some local deity and not the transcendent God?" the LORD asks. —Jeremiah 23:23, NET

> For my thoughts are not your thoughts, neither are your ways my ways, declares the LORD. For as the heavens are higher than the earth, so are my ways higher than your ways and my thoughts than your thoughts. —Isaiah 55:8–9, ESV

> For you, O LORD, are most high over all the earth; you are exalted far above all gods. —Psalm 97:9, ESV

My prayer: Lord, you are holy and above all things. Your essence is far beyond my ability to describe. It is impossible to grasp that you—with all of your greatness, power, love, creativity, *everything* you are—my Creator and King, are not aloof. Remarkably, you made a way for me to be near you. How can I take that in, except with all humility and a tender, grateful heart?

Which way do you more often think of God, being infinitely far above all creation or so close that his Spirit lives in our hearts? Why do you think of him that way?

Immanent/involved

Part of the mystery and miracle of God is that he is transcendent (above all things), and at the same time, he is immanent (involved). He does not stand aloof. He permanently pervades and sustains the universe. Paradoxically, he remains distinct from his creation, and yet is present within it.

> And the Word became flesh and dwelt among us, and we have seen his glory, glory as of the only Son from the Father, full of grace and truth. —John 1:14, ESV

> "And behold, I am with you always, to the end of the age." —Matthew 28:20b, ESV

My prayer: Lord, you are here and involved. Considering your holiness, it is hard to fathom that your answer to humankind's sin was to take the form of a man, dwell here with us, model what we need to know and do, and pave the way to you. You are involved. You are staying right with us. Thank you for being here with me right now.

How do you feel about God being involved in your life, rather than remaining aloof in all of his awesome perfection?

Good

God is good. This simple statement encompasses a huge concept. Unlike in the world, where "good" is the entry-level option of "good, better, best," God's character includes an absolute, the complete absence of evil. He is so full of goodness that it overflows into actions that bless all people, surrounding us with beauty, providing for our needs, and coming to our rescue.

> Oh give thanks to the LORD, for he is good; for his steadfast love endures forever! —1 Chronicles 16:34, ESV

> And behold, a man came up to him, saying, "Teacher, what good deed must I do to have eternal life?" And he said to him, "Why do you ask me about what is good? There is only one who is good. If you would enter life, keep the commandments." —Matthew 19:16–17, ESV

My prayer: Starting from the beginning, Lord, you have shown yourself to be impeccably good, in everything you have made and all that you have done. I praise you for your goodness, and I am so glad that you are good all the time. You never take a break. I know I can trust your actions because they are based on your perfect goodness and love.

How has God's goodness been made plain to you?

Righteous

Righteousness means freedom from guilt or sin, acting in accordance with divine or moral law. Obviously, this is true of God, who is sinless and divine. His holiness leads him to do only what is right. As for humans, no one with unforgiven sin can be in God's presence. When we accept Jesus as our Savior, he covers our sin, and we can stand righteous before God.

> Your righteousness, O God, reaches the high heavens. You who have done great things, O God, who is like you?
> —Psalm 71:19, ESV

> They will proclaim his righteousness, declaring to a people yet unborn: He has done it! —Psalm 22:31

My prayer: My God, the gospel proved that you keep your promises. Your Son is a true reflection of you. He was a model of righteousness, teaching us how to live. Your word tells us that righteousness leads to peace. Yet, as a consequence of our not following Jesus' teaching, this world is full of discord. We can have no peace. Only through your Son's righteousness am I righteous in your sight. He covers my sin before you. I praise and thank you for the huge blessing and peace this brings to me.

In what ways do you strive to be honorable and right-minded in your relationships with other people?

Life

Without God, there is no life, no meaningful activity. God breathes life into each one of us, giving us an opportunity to make a difference in this world. Because of the essence that God established within us, our lifeblood, we desire to live. And it is a sincere act of our will to choose to live for him.

> For as the Father has life in himself, so he has granted the Son also to have life in himself. —John 5:26, ESV

> I call heaven and earth to witness against you today, that I have set before you life and death, blessing and curse. Therefore choose life, that you and your offspring may live, loving the LORD your God, obeying his voice and holding fast to him, for he is your life and length of days, that you may dwell in the land that the LORD swore to your fathers, to Abraham, to Isaac, and to Jacob, to give them. —Deuteronomy 30:19–20, ESV

My prayer: Father of all, you are Life. You were living before you created all life as we know it. You breathed life into me as you made me, and you breathed eternal life into me when I was dead in my sins. Because of your mercy and your power of salvation, I live now and will live forever with you and in you. Hallelujah!

What is one choice you can make to more fully live into the life God gave you?

Wellspring/fountain

A wellspring is the original and bountiful source of something. God was and is the original source of life, and he offers an inexhaustible flow of blessings. Because he is a wellspring, we will never be thirsty for the things we need most in this life.

> For with you is the fountain of life; in your light do we see light. —Psalm 36:9, ESV

> But whoever drinks of the water that I will give him will never be thirsty again. The water that I will give him will become in him a spring of water welling up to eternal life. —John 4:14, ESV

My prayer: My magnificent Lord, you are eternal, everlasting, overflowing with love and mercies. You are the wellspring of life, of grace, of everything I need. Thank you for your inexhaustible supply.

Think of a time when you were really, really thirsty, almost desperate for water. Now, write about how it felt to have that thirst satisfied.

Center

God should be the center of our lives, the focal point for all of our activities. When he is not the center, things become off-balance, sometimes just a little at first, then increasingly so, and we become wobbly. When that happens, we must rearrange our priorities and re-focus on him as the center of our lives.

> Love the LORD your God with all your heart and with all your soul and with all your strength. —Deuteronomy 6:5

> You will seek me and find me when you seek me with all your heart. —Jeremiah 29:13

My prayer: Almighty God, daily I am making you the center of my universe, where my thoughts are focused and where my heart is always anchored. Yes, I stray in thought, and even in deed, but I genuinely desire you to be the center that you deserve to be, in every aspect of my life. And so, I begin each day thankful for another chance to love and serve you more wholeheartedly.

What priorities do you need to shift to strengthen the way you treat God as the focal point in your life?

Plans

God designs, decides on, and arranges everything in advance. In spite of this, our nature is to try to put ourselves in the driver's seat. When we are determined to have our own way, and when that way is not God's way, things begin to go badly for us. But when we realize that his plan is for our good, we return to the right path. God proves himself over and over; trusting him is our best plan.

> LORD, you are my God; I will exalt you and praise your name,
> for in perfect faithfulness you have done wonderful things,
> things planned long ago. —Isaiah 25:1

> "For I know the plans I have for you," declares the LORD, "plans
> to prosper you and not to harm you, plans to give you hope
> and a future." —Jeremiah 29:11

My prayer: Lord, everything about your plan is perfect, every detail. My part is to follow to the leading of your Holy Spirit. Thank you for designing me as I am and for your plan for me that is uniquely for me.

As you look back, how has your life plan been changed to fit with a path that is more aligned with your talents?

Purpose-giver

God has given to each of us many gifts, and one of his gifts is a purpose. He has designed each one of us for a particular purpose. If we are attentive, we see that he has shown us—though likely not the full picture—the reason we exist and why he has created each of us in unique ways. When we act on the opportunities he provides, little by little, we are able to fulfill his good purpose.

> But for this purpose I have raised you up, to show you my
> power, so that my name may be proclaimed in all the earth.
> —Exodus 9:16, ESV

> Now the one who has fashioned us for this very purpose is
> God, who has given us the Spirit as a deposit, guaranteeing
> what is to come. —2 Corinthians 5:5

> . . . who saved us and called us to a holy calling, not because of
> our works but because of his own purpose and grace, which he
> gave us in Christ Jesus before the ages began.
> —2 Timothy 1:9, ESV

My prayer: All-knowing God, it gives me comfort, strength, and incentive to know that you have designed a purpose for me—for me! I see it in the ways that you have gifted me, and I long to share more about you, to help others see you, your greatness, your love, your mercy, and your salvation.

Our job description changes as we go through life. What do you think is your God-given job description at this time?

Relational

How can it be that the God of the universe wants to have a relationship with us? Truly, it is his nature to want to be connected with us. He takes an open, positive, welcoming attitude toward interactions with us. Making that relationship even sweeter, he is generous, patient, and kind.

> Behold, I stand at the door and knock. If anyone hears my voice and opens the door, I will come in to him and eat with him, and he with me. —Revelation 3:20, ESV

> So now we can rejoice in our wonderful new relationship with God because our Lord Jesus Christ has made us friends of God. —Romans 5:11, NLT

My prayer: It is so remarkable, Lord, that you wish to be in relationship with me. You came into a broken world, lived as a man, and died as a complete sacrifice for my sins. I continue to be amazed and am so blessed that I can be in relationship with the Creator/King of the universe.

God reaches out to you to be in relationship. What part do you have in strengthening that relationship?

Abba

This Aramaic term is a tender, child-like name for God as father. It translates to "Daddy" or "Papa." This term of endearment for God was used by Jesus, and as beloved children, we, too, are encouraged to call him "Abba." This perfectly loving God always has his arms wide open to receive us.

> For you have not received a spirit of slavery leading to fear again, but you have received a spirit of adoption as sons and daughters by which we cry out, "Abba! Father!"
> —Romans 8:15, NASB 2020

> And because you are sons, God has sent the Spirit of his Son into our hearts, crying, "Abba! Father!" —Galatians 4:6, ESV

My prayer: Lord, you loved me so much that you invited me to come near, to call you "Daddy." I am so blessed to have the privilege of climbing up onto your lap to be nearer to you and to whisper into your ear what is on my mind. I treasure the intimacy that we have, that I can come to you anytime, and that I will be with you always.

Not all fathers are perfect, of course, but God is. How is it encouraging to you as you think of God in such a tender, personal way?

Attentive

God pays close attention to what we say and do. He is caring, understanding, and accommodating, as he completely sees to our comfort or addresses our concerns.

> The eyes of the LORD are on the righteous, and his ears are attentive to their cry. —Psalm 34:15

> Now My eyes will be open and My ears attentive to the prayer offered in this place. —2 Chronicles 7:15, NASB 2020

My prayer: Lord, because you were close to me, even while I was wandering far away from you, you heard the cry of my heart. You heard not just the cry, but you were sensitive to all of its nuances. You have always known my inmost heart. And you knew that I would have to descend to the point of humility before I cried out to you. Only then would I recognize that you were calling me to be in relationship with you. I praise you for being so attentive to my needs and for caring about every detail in my life.

To what concerns would you like assurance of God's attendance?

Compassionate

Because he loves us, God has a deep awareness of our sufferings and has the desire to relieve them. And his compassions never fail. Besides soothing the hurts inflicted on us, he is compassionate to forgive our sins to relieve that self-imposed burden.

> Have mercy on me, O God, according to your unfailing love;
> according to your great compassion blot out my transgressions.
> —Psalm 51:1b

> You will again have compassion on us; you will tread our sins
> underfoot and hurl all our iniquities into the depths of the sea.
> —Micah 7:19

My prayer: Lord God, Lover of my soul, you know everything about me and the ways in which I have sinned and suffered. Thank you for loving me so much that you pulled me out of that bad place. In doing so, you showed a deep, sweet, loving compassion for your child. Long before I fell in love with you, you loved me with an eternal love. You were ready to forgive my sins, so that I could be in relationship with you.

In what ways does God show compassion for you on a daily basis? And in what ways do you show compassion for those around you?

Inspires

God divinely infuses into our minds things that he wants us to know about him as well as things he wants us to know about ourselves. This infusion could be a creative idea or a godly response to a problem. As he breathes into us, it is often to help us know our purpose. We are to ponder that inspiration and take the next steps along the path he is laying out for us.

> But it is the spirit in man, the breath of the Almighty, that makes him understand. —Job 32:8, ESV

> The angel said to me, "These words are trustworthy and true. The Lord, the God who inspires the prophets, sent his angel to show his servants the things that must soon take place." —Revelation 22:6

> Above all, you must understand that no prophecy of Scripture came about by the prophet's own interpretation of things. For prophecy never had its origin in the human will, but prophets, though human, spoke from God as they were carried along by the Holy Spirit. —2 Peter 1:20–21

My prayer: Lord, I love that "inspiration" is literally your breath that leads me to do what you would have me do. Please help me be sensitive to your leading, aware of your breath within me, carrying me along to do your will.

How has God recently inspired some next steps for you?

Vinedresser

Think of acres of grape vines, neatly arranged, row upon row. That doesn't just happen. A vinedresser painstakingly ties the vines to each trellis, giving the vines support and training them to grow in the right direction. The vinedresser also prunes the vines to maximize the yield. God is the divine Vinedresser. If we let him, God trains us to grow in the right direction, and he works to help us bear abundant fruit.

> [Jesus said,] "I am the true vine, and my Father is the vinedresser. Every branch in me that does not bear fruit he takes away, and every branch that does bear fruit he prunes, that it may bear more fruit." —John 15:1–2, ESV

> [Jesus said,] "Whoever abides in me and I in him, he it is that bears much fruit, for apart from me you can do nothing. —John 15:5, ESV

My prayer: Father God, you are the Vinedresser, the perfect Gardener. Yes, you have pruned me; you have made me grow and bear fruit. I love the Bible verses that refer to Jesus as the vine, because the vine is the central thing. Without the vine, the branches cannot survive. And without the vinedresser, no stem or offshoot can thrive and bear fruit.

What are some examples of the ways God has given you support and training to help you produce more abundant fruit?

Hovers

In the beginning, the Spirit of God hovered, probably using his complete knowledge and focusing his mighty power to create and harmonize all of the universes that we now know exist. Today, God hovers above us, not in a negative, controlling way, but with wisdom, power, and love. He is always near at hand to guide us as we grow.

> The earth was without form and void, and darkness was over the face of the deep. And the Spirit of God was hovering over the face of the waters. —Genesis 1:2, ESV

> In a desert land he found him, in a barren and howling waste. He shielded him and cared for him; he guarded him as the apple of his eye, like an eagle that stirs up its nest and hovers over its young, that spreads its wings to catch them and carries them aloft. —Deuteronomy 32:10–11

My prayer: Lord, it thrills me that your Spirit hovers over me. I know that you are protecting me at all times, as a mother bird protects her young. Without you, I would be vulnerable. While hovering above me, you not only protect me, but you also show me the way to go. You are my Shield and my Sustainer.

Under what circumstances do you think it is helpful to have someone hover over you? And how does it help?

Understands

There is no one who understands us the way God does. He perceives how we think, feel, and behave, and he understands why we think, feel and behave in those ways. Even with all of our imperfections, he dearly loves each of us.

> God understands the way to [wisdom] and he alone knows where it dwells. —Job 28:23

> And you, my son Solomon, acknowledge the God of your father, and serve him with wholehearted devotion and with a willing mind, for the LORD searches every heart and understands every desire and every thought. If you seek him, he will be found by you; but if you forsake him, he will reject you forever. —1 Chronicles 28:9

My prayer: Lord, you know all things. You know my heart; you know my mind; you know what lifts me up and what pushes me down. I am not ashamed nor afraid that you know me so intimately. I am imperfect, quite a stinky sheep at times. But in your eyes I am the beautiful one you created me to be. Thank you for your vision and for your plan for my life.

Have you ever had the luxury of having someone truly understand what is most important to you? If so, how did that feel? If not, how do you think it would feel?

Just/impartial

We can trust that God will always be fair; justice is part of his character. He judges according to what is morally right. He sees into our hearts and minds, and he is faithful to judge equitably and with mercy.

> The works of his hands are faithful and just; all his precepts are trustworthy. —Psalm 111:7, ESV

> God is not unjust; he will not forget your work and the love you have shown him as you have helped his people and continue to help them. —Hebrews 6:10

> Your love, LORD, reaches to the heavens, your faithfulness to the skies. Your righteousness is like the highest mountains, your justice like the great deep. —Psalm 36:5–6a

My prayer: Lord, eternally speaking, and even in day-to-day living, the prospect of separation from you is terrifying to consider. And I know that pure justice would require me to be separated from you because you are too holy for me to be in your presence. But, because of your love for me, as well as your faithfulness, you made a way for me to be with you, through Jesus' cleansing sacrifice. Thank you for this amazing gift that allows me to be in your presence.

Why do you think it is hard for humans to be impartial and judge with complete fairness?

Detests/abhors

While God is a loving God, there are things, intentions, and actions that he regards with disgust, even hatred. With all of the loving, wonderful aspects of God, "abhorrence" sounds so negative, and some people might not believe he is capable of such. But it is in line with his one of his well-known attributes: righteousness.

> There are six things the LORD hates, seven that are detestable to him: haughty eyes, a lying tongue, hands that shed innocent blood, a heart that devises wicked schemes, feet that are quick to rush into evil, a false witness who pours out lies, and a person who stirs up conflict in the community.
> —Proverbs 6:16–19

> The LORD detests the way of the wicked, but he loves those who pursue righteousness. —Proverbs 15:9

My prayer: My gracious Lord, how it must hurt your heart when you see me doing things that you hate. Please help me refrain from the least shadow of them as I live my life for you. I earnestly desire to be righteous in your sight. While I know that I cannot do that in my own strength, I thank you for the righteousness of Jesus that covers all of my sin.

In all honesty, what things do you do—even in some small way—that you detest? What steps can you take to stop doing those detestable things?

Zealous

God is ardently active, devoted, and diligent about us and our welfare in every way. His zeal reflects his fervent love for us and his passionate attention to our good.

> Of the increase of his government and of peace there will be no end, on the throne of David and over his kingdom, to establish it and to uphold it with justice and with righteousness from this time forth and forevermore. The zeal of the LORD of hosts will do this. —Isaiah 9:7, ESV

> O LORD, your hand is lifted up, but they do not see it. Let them see your zeal for your people, and be ashamed. Let the fire for your adversaries consume them. —Isaiah 26:11, ESV

My prayer: Lord, the fact that you—Creator and Sustainer of the universe—are zealous for me and for my wellbeing is so humbling. Your love is unspeakably great. Your power cannot be forestalled. With zeal, you will uphold your plan, and I know that even my very tiny part in your plan is important to you.

What are you zealous about? How can that affect others in a positive way?

Deliverer

In the big picture, when we agree to accept his gift of salvation, God delivers us from eternal peril. He saves us from the clutches of the enemy. On a daily basis, God rescues us from harm or danger. He delivers us from health issues, relationship issues, and many kinds of battles.

> Deliver me from sinking in the mire; let me be delivered from my enemies and from the deep waters. —Psalm 69:14, ESV

> He is my steadfast love and my fortress, my stronghold and my deliverer, my shield and he in whom I take refuge, who subdues peoples under me. —Psalm 144:2, ESV

> For you have delivered my soul from death, yes, my feet from falling, that I may walk before God in the light of life. —Psalm 56:13, ESV

My prayer: Lord, you know that I was in danger so great, and I was not aware of it; in fact, I was completely blind to it. But you loved me so much that you protected me and delivered me. I am so grateful that I can come to you when I do recognize the danger that is around me, and I thank you for protecting me when I am unaware. Because of your love, power, and deliverance, I will not be lost.

From what dire circumstance have you been delivered?

Silences

Our enemy, the devil, tries to speak lies into our lives, with intimidation and hurtful accusations. When we wrestle with the enemy in these situations, we need only to call out to God for his help. God will step in and compel the enemy to be silent.

> In your unfailing love, silence my enemies; destroy all my foes, for I am your servant. —Psalm 143:12

> Let me not be put to shame, LORD, for I have cried out to you; let the wicked be put to shame and be silent in the realm of the dead. Let their lying lips be silenced, for with pride and contempt they speak arrogantly against the righteous. —Psalm 31:17–18

My prayer: Lord, I don't feel that I have earthly enemies, just the one enemy, the accuser. I know that in the end you will silence and destroy him. You have already won that victory. In the meantime, for the daily battle, you have equipped me with your full armor. Thank you for protecting me with your word of truth and for shutting down the enemy's lies.

We have all done things for which we feel ashamed. Even though you've been forgiven, what nags at you that you wish would be silenced?

Wrestles

Like a father with a young son, God will wrestle with us. He will contend with us in a struggle for mastery. While it is futile to wrestle with God, thinking that we will somehow have our own way, these times of grappling can lead us to wisdom and to an understanding that his way is the right way.

> And Jacob was left alone. And a man wrestled with him until the breaking of the day . . . Then [the man] said, "Your name shall no longer be called Jacob, but Israel, for you have striven with God and with men, and have prevailed." —Genesis 32:24, 28, ESV

> Yes, he [Jacob] wrestled with the angel and won. He wept and pleaded for a blessing from him. There at Bethel he met God face to face, and God spoke to him—the LORD God of Heaven's Armies, the LORD is his name! —Hosea 12:4–5, NLT

My prayer: Thank you, Lord, for allowing me to wrestle with you. When I "lost," I won. I won a new relationship with you, here and now. I won access to you. I can boldly approach your throne. I won eternity with you; I won your blessings evermore. In truth, these things that I won were not from my strength, but gifts that you had waiting for me.

With what issue or habit have you wrestled and "lost," then realized that you really came out better for having struggled?

Presses

When the occasion demands it, God really presses down. Exerting a strong, compelling influence on us, he helps us to discern right choices. When he presses down, it is uncomfortable for us if we are going the wrong way. Because he loves us, he wants us to feel the pressure and head in a better direction.

> Behold, I will press you down in your place, as a cart full of sheaves presses down. —Amos 2:13, ESV

> If he shall overturn all things, or shall press them together, who shall contradict him? —Job 11:10, DRB

> You know that under pressure, your faith-life is forced into the open and shows its true colors. So don't try to get out of anything prematurely. Let it do its work so you become mature and well-developed, not deficient in any way. —James 1:3–4, TM

My prayer: Dear Lord, you have lovingly pressed down on me and changed my life. Because you were unwilling that I should perish, you invited me to come to you. You wanted me to desire you and to be willing to let you work to transform me into the person you had in mind when you created me. Your work has already borne some fruit; please Lord, help me be abundantly fruitful for your kingdom.

When we are lovingly pressed, it is an opportunity to become stronger or make better choices. When have you felt pressure—or pressed yourself—to choose a better path?

Demonstrates

Sometimes we need someone to demonstrate why we should believe something. Or, sometimes we need someone to model a concept, so that we can learn or understand. God clearly shows the truth of his word by giving proof, solid evidence. His actions have demonstrated how to live rightly with one another.

> The LORD has demonstrated his holy power before the eyes of all the nations. All the ends of the earth will see the victory of our God. —Isaiah 52:10, NLT

> But those who wish to boast should boast in this alone: that they truly know me and understand that I am the LORD who demonstrates unfailing love and who brings justice and righteousness to the earth, and that I delight in these things. I, the LORD, have spoken! —Jeremiah 9:24, NLT

My prayer: Yes, Lord, you have demonstrated your great love, faithfulness, mercy, patience, power, and more in my life. I am able, therefore, to tell of your excellencies to any who will listen. I pray that your goodness in the lives of others whom you love, protect, and redeem will be identified as originating from you.

What was one of the best things, concepts, or methods that have been demonstrated to you?

Fulfills

God always brings his promises to completion or to reality. We can have confidence that he will achieve everything he has promised. As our loving Provider, he knows our needs and fulfills our desires in precisely the right ways.

> The LORD has done what he planned; he has fulfilled his word, which he decreed long ago. —Lamentations 2:17a

> He fulfills the desires of those who fear him; he also hears their cry and saves them. —Psalm 145:19, ESV

> Not one of all the LORD's good promises to Israel failed; every one was fulfilled. —Joshua 21:45

My prayer: Father, I love that your word tells over and over again how you have fulfilled your promises. This reinforces your character, who you are, and that you do what you say you will do. Promises are covenants. And you are always faithful to fulfill them.

In what ways has God fulfilled his promises to you?

Praiseworthy

God deserves esteem and devotion from all people. He is worthy of all praise and glory. We can praise him in good times and in bad times because we know that his character is excellent in every way. He exercises his sovereignty always with our best interests at heart. He is to be admired above all powers.

> For great is the LORD and most worthy of praise; he is to be
> feared above all gods. —Psalm 96:4

> I called to the LORD, who is worthy of praise, and have been
> saved from my enemies. —2 Samuel 22:4

My prayer: Awesome God, while people admire things and experiences, only you are completely worthy of praise and admiration. Only you are perfect. You are above all, for you created all. Lord, I praise you for all that you are and for all that you have done in my life.

What are your favorite things about God? In what ways do you like to express your praise to him?

Incomparable

How can we compare God to anything or anyone? We can't, and yet we try. It is a human inclination to compare this versus that in order to get a better sense of something (or someone). As we try to compare God, we find that he is matchless; he is without equal in his extent or in his character. And that is reassuring. We need a great big, loving, forgiving, saving, sovereign God.

> Sovereign LORD, you have begun to show to your servant your greatness and your strong hand. For what god is there in heaven or on earth who can do the deeds and mighty works you do? —Deuteronomy 3:24

> Among the gods there is none like you, Lord; no deeds can compare with yours. —Psalm 86:8

My prayer: O God, although I am developing a deeper understanding of you, I know that I have only scratched the surface. Who can know all of your matchless wonders or the full extent of your character and being? I know I never will. I do pray that you will help me continue to draw closer to you. I know that I can thank you in advance for this because it is the desire of my heart as well as in your will.

How can anyone compare God with any "little g" gods who seem to be the focus in our culture?

Omnipresent

God transcends all spatial limitations. Inexplicably, he is both in heaven and on earth at the same time. There is not a place that is devoid of his presence. He is above us, below us, behind us, and beside us, simultaneously.

> For the eyes of the LORD roam throughout the earth, so that he may strongly support those whose heart is completely his.
> —2 Chronicles 16:9a, NASB 2020

> "Can anyone hide from me in a secret place? Am I not everywhere in all the heavens and earth?" says the LORD.
> —Jeremiah 23:24, NLT

> The eyes of the LORD are in every place, keeping watch on the evil and the good. —Proverbs 15:3, ESV

My prayer: My Lord, I love the way that you demonstrated your love for your people Israel when you stayed by them day and night with the cloud and pillar of fire. It is compelling imagery and a reminder of your ever-presence and your guidance. Because you are unchanging, you are present with me as well. This is very comforting. I need not call to a faraway place for you, hoping that you will respond. I know that you are right here with me.

In what ways is it actually comforting that God is always present?

Omniscient

Nothing takes God by surprise. He perceives all things and has foreknowledge of events yet to come. We can be assured that, at all times, he has complete, unlimited awareness, knowledge, and understanding.

> Nothing in all creation is hidden from God's sight. Everything is uncovered and laid bare before the eyes of him to whom we must give account. —Hebrews 4:13

> Before a word is on my tongue you, LORD, know it completely. —Psalm 139:4

My prayer: Lord, you know all things. You know the secrets of my heart, including the motivations that are not in line with your best for me. Yet, from before creation, you chose me to be yours. You know just how to guide me to help me develop more and more into the image of your perfect Son. Thank you for knowing me better than I know myself and for your willingness to transform me so that my life may point to your greatness and love.

In what ways is it reassuring that God knows all things, even things in the future?

Omnipotent/almighty

God has unlimited power. He is easily able to do anything; nothing is impossible for him. His strength knows no bounds. He has ultimate control and influence over people and events, permitting everything that is within his will.

> The One who established the mountains by his strength is clothed in omnipotence. —Psalm 65:6, ISV

> You saw with your own eyes the great trials, the signs and wonders, the mighty hand and outstretched arm, with which the LORD your God brought you out. The LORD your God will do the same to all the peoples you now fear. —Deuteronomy 7:19

My prayer: Almighty God, you have demonstrated time again in my life, and in the lives of others, your immeasurable power and strength. I am so grateful that your great might is infused with your goodness, for without your goodness we would all perish. I stand in awe of you.

How does it change your outlook when you remember that nothing is impossible for Almighty God?

Infinitely-faceted

To call God *multifaceted* would be an understatement. With innumerable definable—and undefinable—aspects, God can be described as infinitely-faceted. We can never get to the end of our discovery of him.

> Oh, the depth of the riches of the wisdom and knowledge of God! How unsearchable his judgments and how inscrutable his ways! —Romans 11:33, ESV

> The purpose of this enlightenment is that through the church the multifaceted wisdom of God should now be disclosed to the rulers and the authorities in the heavenly realms. —Ephesians 3:10, NET

My prayer: Your word, my Lord, speaks of your many facets, and the psalms sing of them, glorifying you for all that you are. In attempting to describe you, I know that I cannot do so entirely. The fullness of you is beyond comprehension. I pray that when any of your attributes are reflected in me, they will be recognized as gifts from you, so that others may direct their gaze to you and come to love and glorify you, too.

When you think of the infinite number of facets, or aspects, of God, what things first come to mind?

Loving

Having shown—and continuing to express—a profoundly tender, passionate affection for all people, God, in turn, asks us to actively focus on loving. He commands us to love him with all our heart, soul, mind, and strength, and to love one another as much as we love ourselves. If we obeyed these commands, the world would be a more just, peaceful place.

> Beloved, let us love one another, for love is from God, and whoever loves has been born of God and knows God. Anyone who does not love does not know God, because God is love.
> —1 John 4:7–8, ESV

> [Jesus said,] "A new commandment I give to you, that you love one another: just as I have loved you, you also are to love one another. By this all people will know that you are my disciples, if you have love for one another." —John 13:34–35, ESV

My prayer: Loving God, the Bible is the greatest love story ever written. In it, you reveal your love for all people and your desire to be with us for all eternity. Through the gift and sacrifice of your Son, you demonstrated the extreme depth of your love. I ask that you help me daily to be more mindful of loving others better, so that my actions may reflect your goodness.

In what ways do you reflect the importance of the love of God in your life?

Architect

In the beginning, God designed, created, and built the world and everything in it. Marvelously, everything in existence holds together, functioning in harmony and interdependently right down to the tiniest subatomic particle. God is the architect who is in perfect command of every detail.

> And let them make me a sanctuary, that I may dwell in their midst. Exactly as I show you concerning the pattern of the tabernacle, and of all its furniture, so you shall make it.
> —Exodus 25:8–9, ESV

> For every house is built by someone, but God is the builder of all things. —Hebrews 3:4

> For he was looking forward to the city with foundations, whose architect and builder is God. —Hebrews 11:10

My prayer: Lord, you are the utmost architect. You made all things from nothing. From nothing. You brought light out of darkness. Only you could conceive of a plan to save me, indeed all people, offering a way out of the just punishment for our sin. Thank you for designing and building me for a special role in your overall blueprint and for supervising my sanctification.

How did God specifically design and build you to contribute to his overall plan?

Originator

An originator is one who creates, who starts or who brings something into being, an inventor, a mastermind. That is a good initial description of God. All things began with him. Appropriately, the Bible starts with these words: "In the beginning, God . . ."

> For as the woman originated from the man, so also the man has his birth through the woman; and all things originate from God. —1 Corinthians 11:12, NASB 2020

> You alone are the LORD. You made the heavens, even the highest heavens, and all their starry host, the earth and all that is on it, the seas and all that is in them. You give life to everything, and the multitudes of heaven worship you. —Nehemiah 9:6

My prayer: Lord, I am awed that your chief purpose for all people is for us to glorify you, and we do this by loving. You are the originator of all love. In 1 John 4:19 I learned that I love because you first loved me. And love leads back to you. I glorify you by loving others and giving thanks to you. May the cycle continue. Love; glorification; more love; glorifying you forevermore.

All things, including love, originated with God. How has love encouraged you to turn your face toward the Lord, the originator of love?

Orderly

Everything about God is harmonious, free from disorder. He established the universe and everything in it in perfect order, and his thoroughly well-ordered systems work together perfectly.

> Thus says the LORD, who gives the sun for light by day and the fixed order of the moon and the stars for light by night, who stirs up the sea so that its waves roar—the LORD of hosts is his name: —Jeremiah 31:35, ESV

> For God is not a God of disorder but of peace—as in all the congregations of the Lord's people . . . But everything should be done in a fitting and orderly way. —1 Corinthians 14:33, 40

My prayer: All-wise Father, you established the perfect order for all things. You demonstrated this before and during creation, and you continue in this way as you sustain the world. You know that a lack of order (chaos) results in a lack of peace, even violence. I thank you for being a God of order, the one who gives me peace through the certainty of your word.

From neat-freak to slob, people vary in the degree of their need for order. How does a sense of order relieve stress in your life?

Chooses/elects

As ruler over all, God gets to choose who is best suited for every role in his kingdom. He elects each person as being the best, most appropriate of the available alternatives. All of his selections throughout the ages have been woven together into a complex, beautiful tapestry according to his purpose.

> For he chose us in him before the creation of the world to be holy and blameless in his sight. In love, he predestined us for adoption to sonship through Jesus Christ, in accordance with his pleasure and will. —Ephesians 1:4–5

> [Jesus said,] "You did not choose me, but I chose you and appointed you so that you might go and bear fruit—fruit that will last—and so that whatever you ask in my name the Father will give you." —John 15:16

My prayer: Lord God, you have chosen me to do your will. You chose to save me. You chose to die to relieve me from the burden of my sins and certain eternal suffering. Please help me to live in the light of your plan for me here on earth, so that you may take pleasure in the "me" that you envisioned and created long ago.

How does it feel to be chosen, selected to be part of something important?

Prepares

God prepares people, places, and circumstances so that his plans will be accomplished and his promises will be fulfilled. He designed us and does countless things to make us ready for his specific purpose.

> But, as it is written, "What no eye has seen, nor ear heard, nor the heart of man imagined, what God has prepared for those who love him." —1 Corinthians 2:9, ESV

> But as it is, they desire a better country, that is, a heavenly one. Therefore God is not ashamed to be called their God, for he has prepared for them a city. —Hebrews 11:16, ESV

My prayer: My dear Lord, you have given me so much. You have prepared me to do important work. You have readied me to share the good news of your love, your salvation, and your kingdom. Thank you for preparing a purpose for me here on earth as well as a place in heaven with you.

How have you seen that God prepared you, the people in your life, or particular circumstances so that his plans would move forward?

Best friend

It may sound overly chummy to call God our best friend, but he is the person we should value above all other friends in our lives. He is someone with whom we can share joys and sorrows, someone we trust, and someone in whom we confide. While "best friend" may sound too familiar, it can be true, all the same.

> Greater love has no one than this, that someone lay down his life for his friends. —John 15:13, ESV

> No longer do I call you servants, for the servant does not know what his master is doing; but I have called you friends, for all that I have heard from my Father I have made known to you. —John 15:15, ESV

My prayer: My Lord, you are my best friend. I run to you with praises and concerns. You are always with me; you are always for me. You speak into my heart for my good. You proved yourself to be the best friend possible before I even recognized it; you were right there protecting me and directing me in the optimal way. Thank you for bringing me out of the darkness and into a deep and lasting friendship with you. Truly, there is none like you.

What does it change if you think of God as your best friend?

Woos

God seeks to win us over. Our hearts are a great treasure to him. He courts us. Others put in a good word about him ("Taste and see that the LORD is good." Psalm 34:8). When he knows our hearts are ready, he asks us to be his, and we lovingly agree.

> But now I am going to woo her—I will bring her out to the desert and I will speak to her heart. —Hosea 2:16, CJB

> He is wooing you from the jaws of distress to a spacious place free from restriction, to the comfort of your table laden with choice food. —Job 36:16

> And when I passed by again, I saw that you were old enough for love. So I wrapped my cloak around you to cover your nakedness and declared my marriage vows. I made a covenant with you, says the Sovereign LORD, and you became mine. —Ezekiel 16:8, NLT

My prayer: Loving God, the fact that the Creator and Sustainer of the universe loves me and draws me to himself is astounding, unfathomable. But you do! Your plan is so filled with love that you are irresistible to me. Thank you for loving me, for seeking to win my heart, and for drawing me to yourself.

When have you been wooed, romanced, or convinced that your suitor was irresistible? How did that feel?

Tender

God shows gentleness toward us, and he expresses his concern and sympathy about the things that are affecting our hearts and lives. He tenderly cares for us and knows just what we need, whether encouragement or redirection. In his love and compassion, he is merciful toward us.

> The LORD is good to all: and his tender mercies are over all his works. —Psalm 145:9, KJV

> And his strong and tender affection is all the more drawn out towards you when he recalls to mind the obedience which all of you manifested by the timidity and nervous anxiety with which you welcomed him. —2 Corinthians 7:15, WEY

My prayer: Lord, you have shown that you are tenderhearted toward me. Your great love has covered all of my sin, and you invited me into a deep and intimate relationship with you. It is a tender relationship in the sweetest way, and I thank and praise you for inviting me to be yours.

How does it affect your thinking about God if you think of him as "tender" toward you?

Mindful

Being omniscient, God is aware of all things, but he is also concerned, mindful about what concerns us. He knows that we are minuscule in the grand scheme of things, but because loves us, he considers us to be important.

> . . . what is mankind that you are mindful of them, human beings that you care for them? —Psalm 8:4

> Just as a father has compassion on his children, So the LORD has compassion on those who fear Him. For He Himself knows our form; He is mindful that we are nothing but dust. —Psalm 103:13–14, NASB 2020

My prayer: Almighty Father, if I am but dust, it is difficult to imagine that you, the great God of the universe, even think about me. You are so magnificent, so vast, so powerful, so *everything* good to and beyond the nth degree. And yet, as I gain a better understanding of you and your unfathomable love, I recognize that you are mindful of me. I am so grateful that I matter to you, that I am valuable in your sight.

How do you respond to the thought that Almighty God is mindful of you?

Keeper

God looks out for us. Yes, we are responsible for the choices we make, but he takes extreme care of us because we are precious in his eyes. He lets us know when we are not on the right track and helps us when we need support.

> The LORD bless you and keep you; the LORD make his face to shine upon you and be gracious to you; the LORD lift up his countenance upon you and give you peace.
> —Numbers 6:24–26, ESV

> Keep me as the apple of your eye; hide me in the shadow of your wings. —Psalm 17:8, ESV

My prayer: Lord, it gives me comfort to know that you are constantly looking out for me. You are the overseer of my soul, and you provide for all of my physical, emotional, and spiritual needs. Without you I would be lost. Thank you for being my Conservator, my Keeper.

In what ways is it a good thing that God is your Keeper?

Tends

God is committed to caring for us at all times. He keeps watch over us and protects us. He even watches over our hearts and minds, freeing us from fear, day and night. He tends to all of our needs, salving our wounds, physical and otherwise, and he helps us heal.

> He will not let your foot slip—he who watches over you will not slumber . . . the LORD watches over you—the LORD is your shade at your right hand. —Psalm 121:3, 5

> The LORD will keep you from all harm—he will watch over your life; the LORD will watch over your coming and going both now and forevermore. —Psalm 121:7–8

My prayer: Loving Father, thank you for your watchcare over me. I was wandering, and although I had lost sight of you, you knew right where I was all along. You kept me from straying too far from the fold. You rescued me when I was in danger, and you brought me back to salve my wounds and heal me spiritually. Thank you, Lord.

In what ways are you blessed to know that God is able to tend to all of your needs?

Watches

God doesn't just glance our way, he observes our lives attentively, as we grow and change. He wants us to know that he is watching, and he cares about how we utilize the time he has given us.

> From his dwelling place he watches all who live on earth—he who forms the hearts of all, who considers everything they do.
> —Psalm 33:14–15

> The LORD said to me, "You have seen correctly, for I am watching to see that my word is fulfilled." —Jeremiah 1:12

My prayer: I know full well, Lord, that you are watching me. As with a child whose parents are watching her, the very fact that you are watching me gives me encouragement, even though sometimes I disappoint you. I want to do my best for you. I do love that you are watching to see that your plan is fulfilled. Thank you for your continual awareness of everything in my life.

What are you working on that you are pleased to have God watch?

Sustains

God strengthens and supports us physically, emotionally, and spiritually. Even as we age, he continues to maintain us. Yes, outwardly we deteriorate, but he continues to sustain our souls.

> Sustain me, my God, according to your promise, and I will live; do not let my hopes be dashed. —Psalm 119:116

> The LORD will sustain him upon his sickbed; In his illness, You restore him to health. —Psalm 41:3, NASB 2020

> Even to your old age and gray hairs I am he, I am he who will sustain you. I have made you and I will carry you; I will sustain you and I will rescue you. —Isaiah 46:4

My prayer: Lord, forgive me when I think that I am self-sustaining. What a folly! All things come from you and are prepared by you to satisfy the vision that you have for me. I do know that. Please help me remember that it is you who sustains me through your gracious goodness and in keeping with your great plan.

In what ways do you rely on others—even on God—to sustain you?

Discerning

God knows us completely; he can tell what is going on in all hearts and minds. In fact, he knows in advance what will be entering our minds. He perceives our thoughts and has a clear view of our motivations.

> Let the evil of the wicked come to an end, but establish the righteous. For you are the righteous God who discerns the inner thoughts. —Psalm 7:9, ISV

> Search me, God, and know my heart; test me and know my anxious thoughts. See if there is any offensive way in me, and lead me in the way everlasting. —Psalm 139:23–24

My prayer: You, Lord, have all wisdom, all knowledge, and you are perfectly able to discern everything about my life, my heart, my soul, even my intentions. Rather than alarming me, it actually comforts me to know that you discern everything about my circumstances because it allows you to show me the way of righteousness.

Nothing can be hidden from God. Is there something in your heart and mind that you need to give over to God so that he can lead you on a better path?

Warns

Because he loves us, God gives us cautionary, even forceful, advice about our plans or our conduct. Sometimes we are willing to change our direction. But if we do not make the change, the truth is that we cannot say later, "Nobody told me."

> Yet the LORD warned Israel and Judah by every prophet and every seer, saying, "Turn from your evil ways and keep my commandments and my statutes, in accordance with all the law that I commanded your fathers, and that I sent to you by my servants the prophets." —2 Kings 17:13, ESV

> See that you do not refuse him who is speaking. For if they did not escape when they refused him who warned them on earth, much less will we escape if we reject him who warns from heaven. —Hebrews 12:25, ESV

My prayer: Loving Father, thank you for coaching and sometimes warning me in whispers, in dreams, and through the words that someone else speaks into my life. In turn, my heart's desire is for my children to hear your love song and be drawn into deeper relationship with you, rather than being jarred by dreadful, urgent "warnings." I pray, too, that each of us will be fully responsive as you reach out to protect us.

When and how have you been cautioned to change a potentially harmful direction?

Defense/defender

God has our ultimate good in mind. He advocates for us, protecting us and defending us from attacks of all kinds.

> You, LORD, hear the desire of the afflicted; you encourage them, and you listen to their cry, defending the fatherless and the oppressed, so that mere earthly mortals will never again strike terror. —Psalm 10:17–18

> It will be a sign and witness to the LORD Almighty in the land of Egypt. When they cry out to the LORD because of their oppressors, he will send them a savior and defender, and he will rescue them. —Isaiah 19:20

My prayer: Lord, I know that you protect me daily from the enemy and from the small "disasters" that are waiting to happen to me. Thank you for being my defender in things large and small.

What small or large disaster were you protected from recently?

Restrains

Most of the time it seems that God keeps his wrath in check, under control. Because he loves us, he would rather guide and discipline us than mete out the just punishment we deserve. Thankfully, God does not give the enemy free rein; God puts some limits on the force of evil in our world and in our lives.

> Surely your wrath against mankind brings you praise, and the survivors of your wrath are restrained. —Psalm 76:10

> For the mystery of lawlessness is already at work. Only he who now restrains it will do so until he [Satan] is out of the way. —2 Thessalonians 2:7, ESV

My prayer: Thank you for your divine restraint, preventing yourself from turning your righteous wrath upon me when you see me engaged in sin. And thank you for restraining the evil one, for protecting me from his clutches. I praise you for being all-powerful and all-good and that you *will* have your way, for your way is always best.

How have you felt God's divine restraint in your life?

Rescues

God is always watching us, his precious people. Sometimes we get into serious trouble. When it is in accordance with his good plan, God steps in and saves us from dangerous or distressing situations.

> Give justice to the weak and the fatherless; maintain the right of the afflicted and the destitute. Rescue the weak and the needy; deliver them from the hand of the wicked.
> —Psalm 82:3–4, ESV

> My whole being will exclaim, "Who is like you, LORD? You rescue the poor from those too strong for them, the poor and needy from those who rob them." —Psalm 35:10

My prayer: Good Shepherd, time and again you have rescued me. I thank you with all my heart. You have rescued me from the evil one and have saved me so that I can spend eternity with you. At times I did not even recognize how bad my situation was, but you knew, and you stepped in and saved me. I praise you for your loving salvation.

When were you rescued from a dangerous situation?

Revives

When we are downtrodden, distraught, demoralized, or just plain exhausted, God gives us new strength, new energy. He revives us by restoring our outlook and breathing new life into our situation when our hope is fading.

> Then we will not turn away from you; revive us, and we will call on your name. —Psalm 80:18

> For we were slaves, but in his unfailing love our God did not abandon us in our slavery. Instead, he caused the kings of Persia to treat us favorably. He revived us so we could rebuild the Temple of our God and repair its ruins. He has given us a protective wall in Judah and Jerusalem. —Ezra 9:9, NLT

My prayer: Lord, as you know, I am a bit stubborn. My natural self wants to go my own way, yet I find comfort, even revival, in your law and in your truth. I know that because of your love, you gave your laws, your wise and loving direction for right living. Thank you for the revival that comes to me as I turn toward obedience, for you have laid out the best path for me.

When you have been distraught or exhausted, what did you find to be effective in reviving you?

Sharpens

Even as God sharpens his sword, he sharpens us. He heightens our senses to be more aware of the needs of others. He hones us, enhancing us for our daily walk. This is not a cosmetic thing; it helps us be more effective as we live for him.

> God is a righteous judge, a God who displays his wrath every day. If he does not relent, he will sharpen his sword; he will bend and string his bow. —Psalm 7:11–12

> If I sharpen my flashing sword and my hand takes hold on judgment, I will take vengeance on my adversaries and will repay those who hate me. —Deuteronomy 32:41, ESV

My prayer: Lord, as I try to sharpen my own skills, I can only go so far. I need your help because I resist further honing. In your great wisdom, you know that I can be better, a better version of myself, a version that is more and more like the "me" you had in mind when you created me. Thank you for sharpening me so that I may exhibit your goodness.

What people or methods sharpen your ability to be at your best for others?

Waits

Although we hate to wait, we can be assured that God's timing is perfect. Sometimes he delays action, waiting until a particular time because all elements in the plan are not yet ready to work together. Later, with the benefit of hindsight, we can see that it was best that he had not answered our prayers according to our timing; he—and we—had to wait.

> Therefore the LORD waits to be gracious to you, and therefore he exalts himself to show mercy to you. For the LORD is a God of justice; blessed are all those who wait for him.
> —Isaiah 30:18, ESV

> After being made alive, he [Christ] went and made proclamation to the imprisoned spirits—to those who were disobedient long ago when God waited patiently in the days of Noah while the ark was being built. In it only a few people, eight in all, were saved through water. —1 Peter 3:19–20

My prayer: Father, how you waited for me! How you loved me, unwilling for me to perish, waiting for me to see that you were there to welcome me into your arms. You exhibited such love and patience! Thank you.

What have you waited for that was tremendously worth the wait? What did you gain during the waiting process?

Harvests

God gathers with joy what has grown or has been produced. The harvest belongs to him because he made it possible. He has enabled all of the right circumstances for the seeds of righteousness to grow. And he provided all that we need to help him in the harvest, but the results are his.

> Therefore pray earnestly to the Lord of the harvest to send out laborers into his harvest. —Matthew 9:38, ESV

> Then another angel came out of the temple and called in a loud voice to him who was sitting on the cloud, "Take your sickle and reap, because the time to reap has come, for the harvest of the earth is ripe." So he who was seated on the cloud swung his sickle over the earth, and the earth was harvested. —Revelation 14:15–16

My prayer: Lord, you have grown me from even before I was a seed. Now is the time of harvest, and you are seeing me produce fruit for you. Even as you are delighting in that harvest, I pray that you will continue to abound in me for your kingdom and your glory.

What good fruit are you producing as you walk through life? How could you be even more fruitful?

Portion/inheritance

In the Bible, a person's *portion* is their inheritance. It is their share of their father's estate. An inheritance is an irrevocable gift with an emphasis on the special relationship between the recipient and the benefactor. God is our benefactor, and he himself is our inheritance. What an incredible gift!

> LORD, you alone are my portion and my cup; you make my lot secure. —Psalm 16:5

> My flesh and my heart may fail, but God is the strength of my heart and my portion forever. —Psalm 73:26

> And the LORD said to Aaron, "You shall have no inheritance in their land, neither shall you have any portion among them. I am your portion and your inheritance among the people of Israel." —Numbers 18:20, ESV

My prayer: Lord, people on earth are concerned with getting their fair share. You are infinite, so a share of you is more than enough. Having you as my inheritance, my portion, is more than I could ever ask for or dream of. And receiving my portion will not diminish that of anyone else. Perfect.

What legacy of eternal value will you be leaving behind? Who will be inheriting that gift?

Triumphant

God orchestrates triumphs every day, and we rejoice when we recognize his victories, small and large. In the end, he will openly display his triumph over the power of evil in our world. The conquered will be shown as "totally defeated."

> Your hand will be lifted up in triumph over your enemies, and all your foes will be destroyed. —Micah 5:9

> But thanks be to God, who in Christ always leads us in triumphal procession, and through us spreads the fragrance of the knowledge of him everywhere. —2 Corinthians 2:14, ESV

My prayer: Lord, each day you lead triumphs over evil. I know that I am able to imagine only a tiny extent of the celebration that will take place in eternity when it is acknowledged that Satan and his forces have been completely destroyed once and for all. Thank you for the promise of your ultimate victory.

What triumph—large or small—have you had lately? How did you give thanks for it?

Radiant/shining

The light of God shines brightly to guide us into all truth a little at a time. Attempting to fully see him would be like walking out of total darkness into dazzling light. Like Saul of Tarsus, the full force of that light would knock us down; it would be far too intense for us to bear. Still, we do long to look into the beautiful radiance of his face, and one day that longing will be satisfied.

> Like the appearance of a rainbow in the clouds on a rainy day, so was the radiance around him. This was the appearance of the likeness of the glory of the LORD. When I saw it, I fell face-down, and I heard the voice of one speaking. —Ezekiel 1:28

> His radiance is like the sunlight; He has rays flashing from his hand, And the hiding of his might is there.
> —Habakkuk 3:4, NASB 2020

My prayer: You are radiant, Lord. When I focus on you, I gain a better understanding of truth, and your light invades my soul in a wonderful, compelling way. Thank you for bringing your beautiful radiance into my life, for shining the light of your love and wisdom onto my path.

Have you seen a person, place, or thing that you would describe as radiant? What was that experience like?

Revered

God deserves to be regarded with awe, adoration, and respectful fear. His holiness is to be admired; his love is to be treasured; his power and authority are to be respected. Because of who he is, and as we learn more and more about him, we have increasing trust and respect for him, and we desire to be obedient to him.

> It is the LORD your God you must follow, and him you must revere. Keep his commands and obey him; serve him and hold fast to him. —Deuteronomy 13:4

> I said, "There is no one like you, LORD. You are great. And you are renowned for your power. Everyone should revere you, O King of all nations, because you deserve to be revered. For there is no one like you among any of the wise people of the nations nor among any of their kings." —Jeremiah 10:6–7, NET

My prayer: Lord, I confess that I do not worship and adore you as deeply and frequently as I should. I know that you are pleased that I love you and have drawn near to you. I do honor, respect, and adore you and am in total awe of you. May your Holy Spirit remind me daily—hourly—of the sense of reverence, awe, and wonder that I should have of the great, great Ruler and Creator of the universe, my own personal Savior who will love me for all eternity.

In what ways do you express reverence? And how do you feel when you are doing it?

Most High

The Hebrew name for God Most High is *El Elyon*. The name acknowledges God's supremacy. His sovereignty is complete, and his power is absolute. Hence, no other god should, or even could, be exalted above him.

> Then they will learn that you alone are called the Lord, that
> you alone are the Most High, supreme over all the earth.
> —Psalm 83:18, NLT

> For the Lord Most High is awesome. He is the great King of all
> the earth. —Psalm 47:2, NLT

My prayer: My great God, you are above all things in heaven and on earth. All things. You are great in every attribute. I praise you for making it obvious through the Scriptures that there is no other god above you and that no other pursuit should take precedence above the pursuit of knowing you.

How do you acknowledge God's position relative to everything else?

Heavenly

God is divine, holy, excellent in the highest degree. He is called our heavenly Father because he is from heaven. Even though he is always present with us, he lives in heaven, a place of perfection and unfathomable beauty and peace.

> Thus says the LORD: "Heaven is my throne, and the earth is my footstool; what is the house that you would build for me, and what is the place of my rest?" —Isaiah 66:1, ESV

> For if you forgive others their trespasses, your heavenly Father will also forgive you. —Matthew 6:14, ESV

My prayer: Holy Father, because you are omnipresent, you inhabit the heavens as well as the earth; yes, you inhabit every place that has been created and beyond. I pray that daily I may make my body, my mind, my heart more appropriate dwelling places for you, my blessed Redeemer and Prince of Peace.

What things do you do to make your world a fitting place for the God of heaven?

Slow to anger

God is so long-tempered. He is the God of the second chance. And the third. And the fourth. And on and on. It is a good thing that he does not treat us as our sins deserve because none of us would make it through childhood. Instead, because he loves us, he welcomes us and helps us learn from our mistakes.

> The LORD is slow to anger and abounding in steadfast love, forgiving iniquity and transgression, but he will by no means clear the guilty, visiting the iniquity of the fathers on the children, to the third and the fourth generation. —Numbers 14:18, ESV

> The LORD is slow to anger and great in power, and the LORD will by no means clear the guilty. His way is in whirlwind and storm, and the clouds are the dust of his feet. —Nahum 1:3, ESV

My prayer: Lord, I live only because you—in your perfect timing, goodness, love, and patience—have been willing to be slow to express your righteous wrath against my many sins. Thank you for your love and for your plan for me. Thank you for preserving me for your purposes.

As you reflect on your life, for which second chances are you most thankful?

Merciful

Mercy means not getting what we deserve. Instead of treating us harshly, as we deserve, God is deeply compassionate in his treatment of us. He is forgiving instead of punishing.

> The Lord passed before him [Moses] and proclaimed, "The Lord, the Lord, a God merciful and gracious, slow to anger, and abounding in steadfast love and faithfulness."
> —Exodus 34:6, ESV

> Answer me, O Lord, for your steadfast love is good; according to your abundant mercy, turn to me. —Psalm 69:16, ESV

My prayer: Lord, when you described yourself to Moses, you mentioned "merciful" first. You proved your great mercy in sending your Son to save sinners like me from eternal punishment for our sins. Indeed, you showed such great compassion for me in my sinful state. I praise you for your love, mercy, and patience. Because of your mercy, I have a new opportunity every day to obey you, serve you, and please you.

When have you expressed mercy—compassion—instead of vindictiveness, unforgiveness, or distain?

Gracious

Grace is getting what we don't deserve. Because of God's character, he is disposed to show kindness and favor toward those who have fallen. Instead of blaming and shaming, he welcomes us, choosing to show us love. God is the giver of grace.

> The LORD is gracious and compassionate, slow to anger and rich in love. —Psalm 145:8

> But in your great mercy you did not put an end to them or abandon them, for you are a gracious and merciful God. —Nehemiah 9:31

My prayer: Lord, when I consider the grace you have demonstrated through the ages, I am dumbstruck. And I know that in my brief moment in time, you have showered me with your grace, love, mercy, and forgiveness. Thank you for loving me first (for I was not capable of loving you first) and for seeing me with the protection of the cloak of your Son's righteousness that covers all of my sin.

When have you been treated with grace—undeserved favor—by someone you expected might give you a hard time?

Source

God is the being from which everything originated. He is the source of all wisdom and knowledge, all love and blessings. He is the source of everything we truly need.

> Yet for us there is but one God, the Father, from whom all things came and for whom we live; and there is but one Lord, Jesus Christ, through whom all things came and through whom we live. —1 Corinthians 8:6

> There I will go to the altar of God, to God—the source of all my joy. I will praise you with my harp, O God, my God! —Psalm 43:4, NLT

My prayer: As the Creator of all things, Lord, you are the source of all things inert as well as everything that lives. Far beyond the things seen and unseen in the ecosystem, you are the source of life, wisdom, joy, strength, and peace. Thank you for being the person from whom I will receive everything I need in this life and in the life to come.

Who or what was the original source of your faith?

Vision

God sees everything, even the things hidden in our hearts. He has the ultimate vision of the future. By providing light to our path, he gives us vision and helps us see the way forward, providing what we need for each next step. Without his light, we are blind.

> But the LORD said to Samuel, "Do not consider his appearance or his height, for I have rejected him. The LORD does not look at the things people look at. People look at the outward appearance, but the LORD looks at the heart." —1 Samuel 16:7

> For now we see only a reflection as in a mirror; then we shall see face to face. Now I know in part; then I shall know fully, even as I am fully known. —1 Corinthians 13:12

My prayer: Lord, I love that you have a vision for me. You see all things, past, present, and future. You know all things and see all of the working pieces of this great puzzle and the way they fit together for my good and your glory. Because you have a unique and perfect vision for me, I have courage, a certainty of step, and the ability to move forward with purpose.

How do you envision yourself one year from now? What must you do to realize that vision or to adjust it in some way?

Foreordains

Being omniscient, God knows everything in advance of its occurrence. For this reason, he is able to appoint people in advance, knowing from long ago everything that is yet to come in their lives. Because he knows these people and the choices they will make, he foreordains that they will live with him in eternity.

> But we speak God's wisdom in a mystery, even the wisdom that hath been hidden, which God foreordained before the worlds unto our glory: which none of the rulers of this world knoweth: for had they known it, they would not have crucified the Lord of glory. —1 Corinthians 2:7–8, ERV

> For whom he foreknew, he also foreordained to be conformed to the image of his Son, that he might be the firstborn among many brethren: and whom he foreordained, them he also called: and whom he called, them he also justified: and whom he justified, them he also glorified. —Romans 8:29–30, ERV

My prayer: Lord, thank you for choosing me, for reserving a place for me to be with you in eternity. I cannot even comprehend such a blessing. Yet knowing who you are, I trust in your promises. Thank you for giving me such assurance of your love and continued protection in this world as well as the sure hope of heaven.

When have you known something in your life was meant to be?

Bestows/gives

God freely hands over to us such things as time, strength, peace, joy, and protection. He is a benevolent God who lovingly gives us everything we need.

> For the LORD God is a sun and shield; the LORD bestows favor and honor. No good thing does he withhold from those who walk uprightly. —Psalm 84:11, ESV

> Look, you will summon nations you did not previously know; nations that did not previously know you will run to you, because of the LORD your God, the Holy One of Israel, for he bestows honor on you. —Isaiah 55:5, NET

My prayer: My generous Lord, you have given so much to me. The greatest gifts are your Son (his teaching, his modeling of how I am to live, his redeeming sacrifice), your Holy Spirit who lives within me, and a place with you in eternity. These gifts are breathtakingly precious and incomparable. Thank you!

What is the best gift you have ever given? What is the best gift you have ever received?

Appoints

In order to accomplish his good plan, God assigns roles to people and determines times and places for many things. It is amazing when we look back at how certain pieces of life's puzzle have fit together. Sometimes things can only be explained by giving God the credit for his divine appointments.

> May the LORD, the God who gives breath to all living things,
> appoint someone over this community to go out and come in
> before them, one who will lead them out and bring them in, so
> the LORD's people will not be like sheep without a shepherd.
> —Numbers 27:16–17

> For God did not appoint us to suffer wrath but to receive salvation through our Lord Jesus Christ. —1 Thessalonians 5:9

My prayer: Lord God, your divine appointments have eternal rewards and consequences. Thank you for appointing various people in my life to help me recognize what you have done for me, so that I would invite you into my heart forever. Thank you for their obedience to your will.

What task or role have you been appointed to fulfill? And how did it feel to be appointed in that way?

Constant companion

Standing steadfastly by our side, God is always with us. He cares about the tiny details in our lives. Accompanying us with firm faithfulness, he is resolved that we will be protected, and he is certain to guide us along the right path.

> Have I not commanded you? Be strong and courageous. Do not be frightened, and do not be dismayed, for the LORD your God is with you wherever you go. —Joshua 1:9, ESV

> When you pass through the waters, I will be with you; and through the rivers, they shall not overwhelm you; when you walk through fire you shall not be burned, and the flame shall not consume you. —Isaiah 43:2, ESV

My prayer: Lord, it gives me great comfort and assurance to know that you are with me always. I feel your presence; it strengthens and reassures me to know that you love me. I know that I can reach out to you at any time, and you will be there.

Who has been your most steadfast companion? In what ways was that relationship important to you?

Personal

God knows everything about our private life, relationships, and emotions. Even knowing all of these things, he still desires a personal, one-on-one relationship with each one of us. When we step into that relationship, we know we will never be the same.

> He [Jesus] said to them, "You are the ones who justify yourselves in the eyes of others, but God knows your hearts. What people value highly is detestable in God's sight." —Luke 16:15

> [Jesus said,] "I am the good shepherd; I know my sheep, and my sheep know me." —John 10:14

My prayer: Dear Lord, I love knowing that you are a personal God and not a faraway God. You have shown your love for me in unimaginable ways. You sought me, and I didn't answer right away, yet you responded when I cried out to you. Indeed, you are never far from me; I know that. I am eternally grateful for your invitation to know you in a personal way.

Reflect on the difference between Jesus being "the Savior of the world" versus your own personal Savior.

Draws us

Because God desires a relationship with us, he comes close to us; he draws near. Lovingly, he also gently pulls us in his direction. He makes it as easy as possible to respond to his invitation; he is right there to welcome us into relationship.

> The LORD appeared to us in the past, saying, "I have loved you with an everlasting love; I have drawn you with unfailing kindness." —Jeremiah 31:3

> [Jesus said,] "No one can come to me unless the Father who sent me draws them, and I will raise them up at the last day." —John 6:44

My prayer: My gracious Lord, I now better understand that I was close to your heart even when my heart was far off, separated from you. You drew me near to you, and I yielded. Then, you cleansed me from the inside out and provided the way for me to be in relationship with you, to be in your beautiful, loving presence. Thank you for drawing me to your side.

What is it about someone that draws you into relationship with them? What drew you to God?

Stoops/condescends

God stoops down from on high to give us the greatest gift of all, eternal life with him. This condescension is certainly beneath his dignity. His great love for us caused Jesus to come down from his high position in heaven, take on human flesh, show us how to live, and then die for our sins.

> Who is like the LORD our God, the One who sits enthroned on high, who stoops down to look on the heavens and the earth? —Psalm 113:5–6

> Have this attitude in yourselves which was also in Christ Jesus, who, as he already existed in the form of God, did not regard equality with God a thing to be grasped, but emptied himself, taking the form of a bond-servant, and being born in the likeness of men. And being found in appearance as a man, he humbled himself by becoming obedient to the point of death: death on a cross. —Philippians 2:5–8, NASB 2020

My prayer: Father, when some people reach a high position in their career, they are so proud that they hold on tight and will not let go for anything. On the contrary, Jesus demonstrated that he was willing to leave his exalted position to save humankind. It is remarkable that his condescension to save me was not done reluctantly. No, he did it obediently, lovingly, and with great compassion, taking into account the wretched state of all of humanity.

How would it feel (or how has it felt) to be befriended or acknowledged by someone who is famous or extremely successful in their field?

Lavishes

By nature, humans are selfish beings, but are we so self-focused and ungrateful that we cannot recognize the great quantities of blessings God has bestowed on us? On a daily basis, he extravagantly showers us with his love, goodness, mercy, forgiveness, and peace.

> But I lavish unfailing love for a thousand generations on those
> who love me and obey my commands.
> —Deuteronomy 5:10, NLT

> How great is the goodness you have stored up for those who
> fear you. You lavish it on those who come to you for protec-
> tion, blessing them before the watching world.
> —Psalm 31:19, NLT

> See what great love the Father has lavished on us, that we
> should be called children of God! And that is what we are! The
> reason the world does not know us is that it did not know him.
> —1 John 3:1

My prayer: Father, you are infinite. Infinitely wise. Infinitely good. Infinitely giving. Therefore, you have been lavish as you have bestowed your love and grace upon me. You have been more generous than I could ask or even imagine. I cannot possibly thank you enough for your extravagant goodness and love.

When have you been extravagant in your giving to someone else? How was that gift received?

Awesome

God is so extremely impressive, he is beyond daunting. He inspires in his people an overwhelming feeling of admiration and reverence for him. When we think about his power and his mighty deeds, we cannot help being awestruck.

> He is the one you praise; he is your God, who performed for you those great and awesome wonders you saw with your own eyes. —Deuteronomy 10:21

> You, God, are awesome in your sanctuary; the God of Israel gives power and strength to his people. Praise be to God!
> —Psalm 68:35

My prayer: Lord, I just cannot fathom your spectacular greatness. The biblical and historical writings about your magnificent deeds help give some dimension to the extraordinariness of your nature, your character, your power, and your being. Yet no amount of documentation, no amount of words, can begin to describe how awesome you are.

What is the most impressive thing you have ever experienced? How did you respond?

Fortress

Calling God a fortress may seem strange, but this imagery indicates that he is our protection, an impenetrable place of fortification against a very powerful enemy. God gives us strength when we are in need or in danger, and he provides encouragement if we are having doubts about how to proceed. He is the solid rock on which we can stand.

> God is my strong fortress, and he makes my way perfect.
> —2 Samuel 22:33, NLT

> The LORD is my rock and my fortress and my deliverer, my
> God, my rock, in whom I take refuge, my shield, and the horn
> of my salvation, my stronghold. —Psalm 18:2, ESV

My prayer: Lord, I am safe in you. I praise you for protecting me from above, below, before, and behind. When trouble approaches, I can run to you—which is possible because you are never far away. I can always count on your protection because you surround me with your love and preserve me for your good purposes.

If you had your own personal (physical) fortress, what would it be like? How would you feel to be within it?

Succors

Like a shepherd, God gives assistance and support in times of hardship and distress, but he goes beyond that. He succors us. *Succoring* means that someone runs to help when another person is in need. God urgently responds to our call for help.

> O remember not against us former iniquities: let thy tender mercies speedily succor us: for we are brought very low.
> —Psalm 79:8, WBT

> For in that he himself hath suffered being tempted, he is able to succour them that are tempted. —Hebrews 2:18, KJV

> But be not thou far off, O LORD: O thou my succour, haste thee to help me. —Psalm 22:19, ERV

My prayer: Lord, I want to always walk in your way, the best way, but I do not always do it. You have shown the way of salvation during times of temptation and distress. In those times, you have assured me that I can run to you for succor. Thank you for being ready to help me during these and all times.

When have you been in a position to immediately respond to someone's urgent call for help?

Jealous

God is fiercely protective and vigilant of his rights and possessions. When we focus on idols—things of this world—or when we put off our worship or study, we are actually cheating God. If we have given ourselves to him, we are his. He has given his own Son for us, so he deserves our love and attention.

> You shall not bow down to them or serve them, for I the LORD your God am a jealous God, visiting the iniquity of the fathers on the children to the third and the fourth generation of those who hate me. —Exodus 20:5, ESV

> They have made me jealous with what is no god; they have pro-voked me to anger with their idols. So I will make them jealous with those who are no people; I will provoke them to anger with a foolish nation. —Deuteronomy 32:21, ESV

My prayer: Loving God, in keeping with your character, it is good and right that you should be jealous of me and any other affections that I have. Lord, I want to be single-minded. I want to have an undivided heart, loving and serving you only. Thank you for protecting our love relationship.

What things take your focus away from God, so that your heart is divided, leaving God with a right to be jealous?

Wrathful

God justly abhors sin. He isn't obliged to wait until judgment day to condemn sinners to eternal punishment; he can express his wrath now by giving the wicked over to their sins. Those who love him and want to be obedient to him can rest assured because he knows all hearts and will spare us.

> For great is the wrath of the LORD that is kindled against us,
> because our fathers have not obeyed the words of this book, to
> do according to all that is written concerning us.
> —2 Kings 22:13b

> See, the storm of the LORD will burst out in wrath, a driving
> wind swirling down on the heads of the wicked.
> —Jeremiah 30:23

> But because of your hard and impenitent heart you are storing
> up wrath for yourself on the day of wrath when God's righteous
> judgment will be revealed. —Romans 2:5, ESV

My prayer: Lord, I know that you withhold your wrath because you are patient and merciful, not wishing anyone to perish. But there comes a point when you decide to let sin run its course and give people over to their sinful ways. Thank you for completely forgiving me for all of my sins. Because you love me and have forgiven me, I will not be an object of your righteous and unrestrained wrath.

Think about a time when you feared you were about to suffer someone's wrath. Now, describe the feeling of relief you had when you realized you would not have to suffer their wrath.

Hides himself

There are times when God purposely makes himself unfindable. Those can be desperate times. He knows our hearts. People who consume their time in running after other gods but then decide that they need God—maybe to help them out of a bind—may find that he has withdrawn. They may find themselves in a world of hurt with no respite.

> Then my anger will be kindled against them in that day, and I will forsake them and hide my face from them, and they will be devoured. And many evils and troubles will come upon them, so that they will say in that day, "Have not these evils come upon us because our God is not among us?"
> —Deuteronomy 31:17, ESV

> No one calls on your name or strives to lay hold of you; for you have hidden your face from us and have given us over to our sins. —Isaiah 64:7

> How long, O LORD? Will you forget me forever? How long will you hide your face from me? —Psalm 13:1, ESV

My prayer: Lord, your word tells of times when you hid yourself. I cannot imagine the complete desolation I would feel if you withdrew and hid yourself from me. It is true that there was a time in my life when I was running away (or attempting to hide) from you, but you were right there, loving me, ready for me to return to your welcoming arms. I praise you for not hiding yourself from me, so that when my heart was ready I did not seek you in vain.

When have you felt completely alone and had the sense that all possible help was just not available to you?

Intervenes

God has a plan for us, and to serve his great purpose, sometimes he decides he must step in to prevent a disaster or alter a result or course of events. Probably most of us can point to times when we believe God intervened to save us from the consequences of bad choices, times when there could be no other explanation except that he had stepped in.

> Those who are left from the kingdom of Judah will take posses-sion of it. By the sea they will graze, in the houses of Ashkelon they will lie down in the evening, for the LORD their God will intervene for them and restore their prosperity.
> —Zephaniah 2:7, NET

> You gave me life and favor, and your intervention watched over my spirit. —Job 10:12, NET

My prayer: I look back, Lord, and I see many times when you have inter-vened to literally save my life, calling me to a safe place. Thank you for being willing to step in and alter the seemingly inevitable course of events. By stepping in, you demonstrated your all-knowing love for me and your as-surance that you have a purpose for me.

Describe a time when God stepped into your life to save you from the conse-quences of bad choices or to prevent a disaster.

Hides us

Naively or foolishly we can allow ourselves to walk in places where bad things can happen. Sometimes God must hide us from dangerous people or take a spotlight from us to conceal and protect us. God has his best for us, and he is not willing for evil to befall us.

> In the cover of your presence you hide them from the plots of men; you store them in your shelter from the strife of tongues.
> —Psalm 31:20, ESV

> For he will hide me in his shelter in the day of trouble; he will conceal me under the cover of his tent; he will lift me high upon a rock. —Psalm 27:5, ESV

My prayer: Lord, I am sure that I do not know how many, many times you have hidden me from the view of others who had evil intent against me. Thank you for continuing to lovingly hide me in the shadow of your wings.

Can you think of a time when you were "miraculously" taken out of the spotlight, thereby being concealed or protected?

Reproves

When God disapproves of our attitudes, actions, or inaction, he loves us enough to scold us. His reproofs can be gentle nudges or something less subtle, and he does it to set us back on the right course.

> Behold, blessed is the one whom God reproves; therefore despise not the discipline of the Almighty. —Job 5:17, ESV

> My son, do not despise the LORD's discipline or be weary of his reproof, for the LORD reproves him whom he loves, as a father the son in whom he delights. —Proverbs 3:11–12, ESV

My prayer: Loving Lord, from childhood, I have not easily received any reproof, perhaps for fear of rejection. If I received one disapproving look, I felt devastated. Now I can see that your reproof is loving, and I need not fear your rejection. Thank you for transforming my mind and heart and for showing me that when you reprove me, you are trying to correct my ways so that I may become the person you designed me to be.

When did you realize that a reproof, a scolding, was actually good for you because it moved you in a better direction?

Softens

When the time is right, God softens our hearts to help them become more sympathetic and responsive, rather than egocentric and critical. He himself softens the soil of our hearts to receive the seeds that are planted and to allow those seeds to grow.

> And I will give you a new heart, and I will put a new spirit in you. I will take out your stony, stubborn heart and give you a tender, responsive heart. —Ezekiel 36:26, NLT

> They who dwell in the ends of the earth stand in awe of Your signs; You make the sunrise and the sunset shout for joy . . . You water its furrows abundantly, You settle its ridges, You soften it with showers, You bless its growth. —Psalm 65:8, 10, NASB 2020

My prayer: Dear Lord, my heart was in danger of becoming hardened. Somehow, I had missed your loving message of grace and salvation. I had been deceived, thinking that I was "basically a good person," good enough to have heaven in my future. At the same time, I was dedicated to looking out for my own interests. Yet you knew that something of my tender spirit remained. You "watered" that soil, transformed my heart, and changed my focus on myself to a focus on you. I praise you for showing me your truth.

What person do you know who needs to have their heart softened? How do you think that can happen?

Speaks

God talks to us in order to advise us, reprove us, or convey information we need to know. Sometimes he speaks in an audible voice, sometimes through Scripture, and sometimes through the words uttered by another person. He knows how to speak so that we will listen.

> Then the LORD said to Moses, "Tell the Israelites this: 'You have seen for yourselves that I have spoken to you from heaven.'"
> —Exodus 20:22

> I will proclaim the LORD's decree: He said to me, "You are my son; today I have become your father." —Psalm 2:7

> In the past God spoke to our ancestors through the prophets at many times and in various ways, but in these last days he has spoken to us by his Son, whom he appointed heir of all things, and through whom also he made the universe. —Hebrews 1:1–2

My prayer: Lord, I know that you speak to me in various ways. Sometimes I am more sensitive and more willing to listen than at other times. Please tenderize my heart, so that I can hear you always. Strengthen me, Lord, so that I will obey your wise and loving words.

God communicates with people in many ways; sometimes it is just "a sense." How may God have spoken to you?

Proves

God has clearly demonstrated the truth of his word through fulfilling prophecy. He does not have to argue his case; he evidences his love to us day by day through the many blessings we receive.

> But the LORD Almighty will be exalted by his justice, and the holy God will be proved holy by his righteous acts.
> —Isaiah 5:16

> The LORD our God truly has displayed his glory and power, for we heard him from out of the fire today. We have witnessed how God spoke to human beings, yet they lived.
> —Deuteronomy 5:24, ISV

> Every word of God proves true; he is a shield to those who take refuge in him. —Proverbs 30:5, ESV

My prayer: Lord, my God, you have proven yourself to me so many times. I have seen that you are true, righteous, holy, loving, merciful, and faithful. I need no further proof. You are my refuge and strength, my Lord and Savior.

When has someone set out to prove something to you? Were you convinced? Why or why not?

Solves

If we go to God with a problem, sometimes he provides an explanation; with his help, we can understand the reason or can see our way through. Sometimes he solves the problem. When he does either of these things, it reinforces to us that we can bring any problem to him.

> And this is the confidence that we have toward him, that if we ask anything according to his will he hears us. And if we know that he hears us in whatever we ask, we know that we have the requests that we have asked of him. —1 John 5:14–15, ESV

> Ask, and it will be given to you; seek, and you will find; knock, and it will be opened to you. For everyone who asks receives, and the one who seeks finds, and to the one who knocks it will be opened. —Matthew 7:7–8, ESV

My prayer: Lord, you know the problems of the human condition, and you showed your love for us by providing the solution: Jesus. Truly, he is the only solution. I am so grateful that I can come to you with my problems large and small. Thank you for not shooing me away and calling me foolish, instead you love me and show me the way.

What problem would you like to have solved? What can you do to approach that challenge?

Magnificent

The natural world is impressively beautiful, elaborate, and spectacular. And God, who created all of it, is even more magnificent. Through nature, he invites us to have a peek at his power and creativity and to bask in the wonder of him.

> O LORD, our LORD, how magnificent is your reputation throughout the earth! You reveal your majesty in the heavens above! —Psalm 8:1b, NET

> Or has any god ever taken for himself one nation out from another nation with testings, signs, wonders, wars, awesome power, and magnificent, terrifying deeds as the LORD your God did in Egypt before your eyes? —Deuteronomy 4:34, ISV

My prayer: Lord, you know that I don't have words to describe your magnificence. No human does. But I know with all of my being that every aspect of your perfect character is far beyond my wildest imaginings. I pray that even a glimpse of your magnificence will serve as a compelling invitation to those who do not yet know you.

What have you seen or experienced that you would describe as magnificent?

Unchanging/immutable

The fact that God is immutable, consistent over time, gives us assurance that everything he has promised is true. People are fickle; cultures shift, but we need not have any misgivings about God because his perfect character is unchanging.

> God is not man, that he should lie, or a son of man, that he should change his mind. Has he said, and will he not do it? Or has he spoken, and will he not fulfill it? —Numbers 23:19, ESV

> God, by whom you have been marked out in his purpose, is unchanging and will make it complete.
> —1 Thessalonians 5:24, BBE

> Every good and perfect gift is from above, coming down from the Father of the heavenly lights, who does not change like shifting shadows. —James 1:17

My prayer: Lord, knowing that you do not change and will not change gives me such assurance. You were perfect in all of your creation and all of your judgments from the beginning, and your constancy and consistency give me confidence to entrust everything to you.

What unchanging thing gives you comfort or confidence?

Alpha

God and Jesus existed before the beginning, and together with the Holy Spirit, they created all things, visible and invisible. Appropriately, the first letter of the Greek alphabet, *alpha*, is used to designate "first" or "the beginning" and may be a first step in describing God. He is the ultimate Alpha; he is our Leader, Ruler, and Maker.

> When I saw him, I fell at his feet as though dead. Then he placed his right hand on me and said: "Do not be afraid. I am the First and the Last. I am the Living One; I was dead, and now look, I am alive for ever and ever! And I hold the keys of death and Hades." —Revelation 1:17–18

> He said to me: "It is done. I am the Alpha and the Omega, the Beginning and the End. To the thirsty I will give water without cost from the spring of the water of life. —Revelation 21:6

My prayer: Awesome God, you were the First. The First before creation, and you will be First forevermore. You represent the beginning of my new life; you invited me to live with you and in you. Please help me as I try to continually put you first in my mind, heart, actions, speech, and motivations.

There is a saying: "First things first." What is first in your day? And what takes first priority in your day-to-day living? Should any of that be reordered?

Before

Being infinite, God has always existed. Because humans are finite, it is impossible for our minds to truly grasp God's "before-ness." He existed before time and space, before the beginning of the world. Describing him in a finite, positional way, he is always going before us, looking out for us, showing us the way.

> For in him [God the Son] all things were created: things in heaven and on earth, visible and invisible, whether thrones or powers or rulers or authorities; all things have been created through him and for him. He is before all things, and in him all things hold together. —Colossians 1:16–17

> The LORD created me at the beginning of His way, before His works of old. From eternity I was established, from the beginning, from the earliest times of the earth.
> —Proverbs 8:22–23, NASB 2020

My prayer: Ever-present God, you are Creator of everything, hence, you had to exist before the beginning of time. Because you are omniscient, every one of my days was known by you before even one of them came to be. I am assured that you are always "before" me, right in front of me, knowing my every step. I know that you protect me and guide me, and I trust in you completely.

Picture a day without God going before you. How do you feel?

Ancient of Days

Attiq-Yomin (Ancient of Days) is one of the Aramaic names for God. The Ancient of Days has imagery of white clothing and hair like pure wool (purity) and a throne of fiery flames (judgment). He is worthy of reverence and respect.

> As I looked, thrones were set in place, and the Ancient of Days took his seat. His clothing was as white as snow; the hair of his head was white like wool. His throne was flaming with fire, and its wheels were all ablaze. —Daniel 7:9

> Yes, and from ancient days I [the LORD] am he. No one can deliver out of my hand. When I act, who can reverse it? —Isaiah 43:13

My prayer: Ah, Sovereign God, a hushed awe comes over me when I contemplate you as the Ancient of Days. I tremble at the thought of being before your throne. You are to be revered. You are wise and good and righteous and powerful, and you will reign with purity and judgment over your kingdom forever and ever.

What very old person have you revered? Why did you revere them?

Creative

Obviously, God has displayed the ultimate in creativity by designing and bringing into being everything that exists. His creativity continues to be shown in the stunning splashes of natural beauty and the mind-boggling intricacies that surround us day by day, season upon season. God even demonstrates creativity in the way he employs people (or animals!) to deliver a message.

> God created everything through him [Jesus], and nothing was created except through him. —John 1:3, NLT

> The angel of the LORD asked him, "Why have you beaten your donkey these three times? I have come here to oppose you because your path is a reckless one before me. The donkey saw me and turned away from me these three times. If it had not turned away, I would certainly have killed you by now, but I would have spared it." —Numbers 22:32–33

My prayer: O, Lord, I am in awe of how marvelously creative you were in the beginning and are still today, both in broad strokes as well as in infinite detail. What a wonder, the way you designed all things and continue to be involved in creative ways in order to make all things to work together.

In your experience, what aspect of God's creativity has most boggled your mind?

Precise

God is particular about details. Precise. Exact. He measured each aspect of space, set boundaries for our planet's waters, and established time itself. And all of his specifications continue to work together. When he gave directions to people like Noah and others, he was specific. In everything, his precision is for our good.

> So make yourself an ark of cypress wood; make rooms in it and coat it with pitch inside and out. This is how you are to build it: The ark is to be three hundred cubits long, fifty cubits wide, and thirty cubits high. —Genesis 6:14–15

> As for God, his way is perfect: the word of the LORD is precise: a shield to all those that wait in him. —Psalm 18:30, JUB

My prayer: Lord, because of your precision, everything in the universe holds together. An example of the precision of your direction was the exact way Noah was to build the ark. One might wonder why that level of detail was captured in the Bible. Then, you demonstrated why following your commands results in our good. We come to understand that you wanted the ark built in a particular way so that it could withstand the coming crisis, saving your chosen people and animals. I need not question your direction for my walk. You have demonstrated that your way is perfect, so I can always trust it.

Why do you think God's precision—in anything—is beneficial?

Orchestrates

God is the maestro of our lives. He directs or arranges the elements of a given situation to produce his desired effect. Sometimes he does this surreptitiously, and when we recognize his hand in our lives, we are twice blessed.

> The lot is cast into the lap, but its every decision is from the LORD. —Proverbs 16:33, ESV

> You see, at just the right time, when we were still powerless, Christ died for the ungodly. —Romans 5:6

My prayer: All-knowing God, you are the great mastermind. I am so thankful that your ways are not my ways. You have a plan and a purpose for me. You knew all things beforehand; you allowed and directed things, even details, to come together so that the outcome would be harmonious. Thank you for your perfect plan. Help me hear your voice as you direct my steps, Lord, so that I may give you the best I have to offer.

Have you ever experienced being under the direction of a maestro? What difference did they make in the outcome or performance of the group?

Initiator

God initiated everything, from the design and creation of our world to his relationship with every individual since Adam and Eve. He is the divine and eternal prime mover. In wisdom, love, and grace, he reaches out to us.

> This is love: not that we loved God, but that he loved us and sent his Son as an atoning sacrifice for our sins . . . We love because he first loved us. —1 John 4:10, 19

> We do this [run with endurance the race God has set before us] by keeping our eyes on Jesus, the champion who initiates and perfects our faith. Because of the joy awaiting him, he endured the cross, disregarding its shame. Now he is seated in the place of honor beside God's throne. —Hebrews 12:2, NLT

My prayer: You, Lord, initiated all things, including our love relationship. You designed me; you called me to come to you. You are the wonderful initiator who began the world and set out a path for me. Thank you!

All it takes is one person to make the first move in beginning a relationship. In what ways did God initiate a relationship with you?

Wills

The purpose of God is never thwarted; everything will inevitably work out the way he intends. He has a good purpose for everyone, and all things fit together in his perfect plan, so it is best when we are obedient to his will.

> In the Messiah we were also chosen when we were predestined according to the purpose of the one who does everything that he wills to do. —Ephesians 1:11, ISV

> All these are empowered by one and the same Spirit, who apportions to each one individually as he wills.
> —1 Corinthians 12:11, ESV

> Instead you ought to say, "If the Lord wills, we will live and do this or that." —James 4:15, ESV

My prayer: God Almighty, there are things that are inevitable, and they are in your will, your perfect will. Thank you for making me feel confident that, even when things look bleak, you have already won the victory. Everything is, and will be, according to your good and perfect will.

As you reflect on important things in your life, can you identify something that was definitely God's will for you? What was it? Does it give you comfort to know that he desires good for you?

Reaches down

Picture the very highest, loftiest place in the universe, a place of extraordinary beauty, complete satisfaction, and utmost comfort, a place of perfect goodness and sovereign power. God is there. And yet he extends his hand to us. He reaches down to take hold of us, especially when we are in desperate need.

> He reached down from on high and took hold of me; he drew me out of deep waters. He rescued me from my powerful enemy, from my foes, who were too strong for me.
> —Psalm 18:16–17

> He reaches down from heaven and saves me, challenging the one who tramples me. *Selah*. God sends his faithful love and truth. —Psalm 57:3, HCSB

My prayer: Lord, as in the days of the writers of the psalms, you still reach down to help, to revive the lowly. That's what I was before you rescued me, lowly and threatened with destruction. You not only rescued me, you made me your child. This is love, that you left your lofty, separated, holy place and reached down to invite me to be beloved in your family.

In what way have you recently extended a hand to help someone who was downtrodden or in need? How was your offer of help received?

Invites

Because he wants to have a relationship with us, God invites us into his presence, kindly requesting that we participate in his family. We don't have to get all dressed up to answer his invitation; we can be ourselves. He knows us as we are.

> Give ear and come to me; listen, that you may live.
> —Isaiah 55:3a

> The Spirit and the Bride say, "Come." And let the one who hears say, "Come." And let the one who is thirsty come; let the one who desires take the water of life without price.
> —Revelation 22:17, ESV

My prayer: O Lord, my God, you have made so many invitations throughout Scripture and in my own life. Thank you for unplugging my ears and opening my eyes to the beautiful, marvelous, glorious invitation to walk with you in this life and to be with you throughout eternity.

What is the most amazing invitation you have received and accepted?

Pursues

With unfaltering love and a complete understanding of our flaws, God still comes after us, steadily pursuing a relationship with us. Some people feel it is necessary to keep running away from him. Others are willing to let the pursuit end, and they give themselves over to him with a reassured "Now I know I'm right where I need to be" sigh. And that opens the way for the beautiful relationship to grow.

> Surely your goodness and unfailing love will pursue me all the
> days of my life, and I will live in the house of the LORD forever.
> —Psalm 23:6, NLT

> But with an overflowing flood he will make a complete end
> of the adversaries, and will pursue his enemies into darkness.
> —Nahum 1:8, ESV

My prayer: My Lord and my Shepherd, you have not only invited me, you have pursued me, even as I was wandering off. You knew what was best for me. You had a plan for me, and you pursued me with an everlasting love. Thank you for being with me wherever I am and for protecting me as someone who is precious to you.

While it does not sound very dignified for Almighty God to pursue us, he knows his plans for us. In what way(s) has God pursued you? And, if you have given yourself over to him, why?

Confessor

A dear and forgiving confessor, God listens as we own up to our sins; he pardons us and provides spiritual counsel. It is good for us to acknowledge that we have wronged someone, particularly God. Confession relieves a burden that weighs us down, and it helps us recognize how to avoid the problem the next time. And, after we have confessed and see a better way forward, the healing can commence.

> Finally, I confessed all my sins to you and stopped trying to hide my guilt. I said to myself, "I will confess my rebellion to the LORD." And you forgave me! All my guilt is gone.
> —Psalm 32:5, NLT

> If we confess our sins, he is faithful and just and will forgive us our sins and purify us from all unrighteousness. —1 John 1:9

My prayer: Father, you do search my heart, and you know that I carry a heavy burden for my sins. Please forgive me for not letting go of some of them. Your word assures me that you have relieved this burden through the worthy sacrifice of Christ, my Savior. Thank you for forgiving me and "remembering my sins no more."

Are you avoiding confessing something to the Lord? Why? How does it help to know that he will completely forgive you?

Precious

After we fall in love with God, we grieve for the time that we wasted when we had not yet reached out to him in love. God becomes our treasure. He is someone who is precious to us, deeply loved, and not to be treated carelessly.

> The law from your mouth is more precious to me than thousands of pieces of silver and gold. —Psalm 119:72

> For you know that it was not with perishable things such as silver or gold that you were redeemed from the empty way of life handed down to you from your ancestors, but with the precious blood of Christ, a lamb without blemish or defect.
> —1 Peter 1:18–19

My prayer: Father, you are precious to me, more and more precious every day. As I walk with you and delve into your word, I gain a greater understanding of who you are and what you have done for me. You are a treasure to me; your word is a rare gift; your Son is beyond anything that anyone could wish for. Thank you, too, dear Lord, that your word says that I am *your* treasure. I cannot find a way to adequately articulate how special it is that you have invited me into an eternal relationship with you.

What treasures do you have? Why do you consider them treasures? In what ways is God precious to you?

Miracle-worker

The Bible has documented many of God's miraculous feats. He is still work-ing miracles today. He does not do it to show off, like some kind of magi-cian; he does it to further his purpose. He has sovereign control over the universe and is able to do far beyond what we can ask or imagine.

> The LORD replied, "Listen, I am making a covenant with you in the presence of all your people. I will perform miracles that have never been performed anywhere in all the earth or in any nation. And all the people around you will see the power of the LORD—the awesome power I will display for you."
> —Exodus 34:10, NLT

> Come and see what our God has done, what awesome miracles he performs for people! —Psalm 66:5, NLT

> You are the God who performs miracles; you display your power among the peoples. —Psalm 77:14

My prayer: My Lord and Savior, I know full well that nothing is too dif-ficult for you. Indeed, you have worked miracles throughout history. Thank you for the way you have worked wonders in my life, and especially when I specifically asked. I pray that I may be bold to ask for a miracle—not to test you, my God and King—so that others may see your power and come to know you.

What miracle(s) has God performed in your life or the life of a loved one?

Pours

God pours love and grace into each one of us. The Bible speaks frequently about his pouring out his Spirit into the hearts of people who will accept him. He knows just what we need, and he is willing to pour his refreshing living water into the one who is thirsty for him.

> And hope does not put us to shame, because God's love has been poured out into our hearts through the Holy Spirit, who has been given to us. —Romans 5:5

> Therefore this is what the Sovereign LORD says: My anger and my wrath will be poured out on this place—on man and beast, on the trees of the field and on the crops of your land—and it will burn and not be quenched. —Jeremiah 7:20

My prayer: Bountiful Father, thank you for so richly pouring your love, and not your wrath, into my life. Please make me a vessel that will, in turn, pour your love into the lives of others and that this will be seen as a blessing from you.

What unexpected blessings has God poured into your life? Did you recognize it at the time?

Surrounds

There are so many words similar to *surrounds* that describe how God covers us completely: wraps, envelops, enfolds, cocoons, encompasses, swathes. Regardless of the way we describe his encircling of each one of us, we can praise him for the warm sense of security that he offers.

> Surely, LORD, you bless the righteous; you surround them with your favor as with a shield. —Psalm 5:12

> You are my hiding place; you will protect me from trouble and surround me with songs of deliverance. —Psalm 32:7

> You hem me in, behind and before, and lay your hand upon me. —Psalm 139:5, ESV

My prayer: You, Lord, envelop me with love and protection, and you lead me to a place of peace. I know that you are surrounding me at all times, swaddling me with your love, and I am so grateful for the security and peace your favor brings.

In what ways do you sense God surrounding you? How does that feel?

Shield/hedge

As a defense against our formidable enemy, God places a barrier or boundary around those who love him. His barricade is impenetrable, and it gives a remarkable sense of peace to know that he is protecting us.

> Have you not put a hedge around him and his household and everything he has? You have blessed the work of his hands, so that his flocks and herds are spread throughout the land.
> —Job 1:10

> But you, LORD, are a shield around me, my glory, the One who lifts my head high. —Psalm 3:3

> He holds success in store for the upright, he is a shield to those whose walk is blameless, for he guards the course of the just and protects the way of his faithful ones. —Proverbs 2:7–8

My prayer: Loving Lord, I know that you guard me as one of your beloved but vulnerable chicks, gathered under your great wing. I rest in your shadow, knowing that you are watching out for my good. The enemy seeks to swoop in and wreak his havoc, but I am safe with you. Thank you for shielding me from the evil one. I trust in you.

Under what circumstances have you needed God to put a hedge of protection around you or your loved ones? Then what happened?

Subdues/stills

One way or the other, sooner or later, God stills the chaos in our lives. If we come to him, he grants us peace as he subdues the enemy who caused havoc when sin ruled our lives. If we do not come to the Lord, he may continue to pursue us, or he may let sin run its course. Eventually, he will still our rebellion.

> Oh, that my people would listen to me! Oh, that Israel would follow me, walking in my paths! How quickly I would then subdue their enemies! How soon my hands would be upon their foes! —Psalm 81:13–14, NLT

> You have armed me with strength for the battle; you have subdued my enemies under my feet. —2 Samuel 22:40, NLT

> He stilled the storm to a murmur, and the waves of the sea were hushed. —Psalm 107:29, HCSB

My prayer: Lord, you can still the greatest storm within me or in the outside world, for all things are subject to you. All that is within me is at peace because you have overcome sin, and I wait in joyous anticipation and confidence of the final proof of your victory, when the enemy is subdued once and for all, unable to stir up evil or rebellion against you any longer.

Can you describe your personal storm that God has stilled? What storms are you currently facing that require Almighty God's intervention to subdue or stop completely?

Satisfies

God more than meets our expectations, needs, and desires. He knows our every need and satisfies us beyond our imagining. The bread and wine of communion (symbols of Jesus' body and blood) remind us that only he can satisfy our spiritual hunger and thirst.

> . . . for he satisfies the thirsty and fills the hungry with good things. —Psalm 107:9

> The LORD will guide you always; he will satisfy your needs in a sun-scorched land and will strengthen your frame. You will be like a well-watered garden, like a spring whose waters never fail. —Isaiah 58:11

My prayer: Loving Father, you satisfy me in every way. Food, water, shelter, and loving relationships satisfy me outwardly, and your word and your truth satisfy the needs of my heart. Thank you for knowing exactly what I need and for always being faithful, yes, abundant, in your provision.

What things do you find to be satisfying? For what things do you hunger or thirst?

Spotlights/exposes

God sometimes shines an intense light on certain things in our lives to direct us to examine our motivations, our actions, or even our inaction. When he spotlights those certain things, it exposes what we need to really see; it reveals something that is true and may even be objectionable. And it points us in a better direction.

> The LORD's light penetrates the human spirit, exposing every hidden motive. —Proverbs 20:27, NLT

> For God, who said, "Let light shine out of darkness," made his light shine in our hearts to give us the light of the knowledge of God's glory displayed in the face of Christ. —2 Corinthians 4:6

My prayer: Lord, I am so grateful that your word spotlights Jesus, modeling for me how to love. You know all of the secrets of my heart, all of my motives, everything about me, and you direct my attention to Jesus. Thank you for exposing to me the things that I must address to be more like him. Thank you for this deep, convicting love.

Have you ever had an unlovely motivation, action, or word exposed to others? What good came out of the exposure?

Curses

When God righteously declares that calamity will fall upon someone, it is dreadful, horrific. We are blessed to have a choice to love, honor, and obey him. When we make that choice, he saves us from destruction.

> [God said to Abram,] "I will bless those who bless you, and whoever curses you I will curse; and all peoples on earth will be blessed through you." —Genesis 12:3

> "If you do not listen, and if you do not resolve to honor my name," says the LORD Almighty, "I will send a curse on you, and I will curse your blessings. Yes, I have already cursed them, because you have not resolved to honor me." —Malachi 2:2

My prayer: Lord, there is no more potent curse than the one that you put forth and no more significant antidote than salvation through your Son, Jesus. I am overwhelmed with thanks that through him you have saved me from the curse of sin and ultimate destruction.

Have you ever known a person who seemed to have a curse hanging over them? If so, how was that curse resolved?

Able

God has the power, the skill, and the means to do anything. To doubt in the slightest that he *can* do something is a grossly uninformed view. He is able, infinitely able. The key is to ask according to his will and to trust that he *will* choose to do that which we ask.

> Yet he did not waver through unbelief regarding the promise of God, but was strengthened in his faith and gave glory to God, being fully persuaded that God had power [was able] to do what he had promised. —Romans 4:20–21

> Now to him who is able to do immeasurably more than all we ask or imagine, according to his power that is at work within us, to him be glory in the church and in Christ Jesus throughout all generations, for ever and ever! Amen.
> —Ephesians 3:20–21

My prayer: Almighty God, to say that you are able sounds so inadequate. Of course, you are able. You are able to do anything that aligns with your good purpose. I know that I can rely on your abilities in all things. Thank you for that assurance.

When something important seems impossible, what can you do to rest on God's ability to bring it to the conclusion that you hope for?

Buffers

We know that life is not all butterflies and rainbows. Look around. It is obvious that we live in a broken world. Yet when we are facing something terrible, God often acts as a buffer to reduce or moderate the impact of it. He knows what we can bear and is kind to relieve the rest.

> Though I walk in the midst of trouble, you preserve my life. You stretch out your hand against the anger of my foes; with your right hand you save me. —Psalm 138:7

> "Because the poor are plundered and the needy groan, I will now arise," says the LORD. "I will protect them from those who malign them." —Psalm 12:5

My prayer: Merciful Father, you help me see that you are all that matters, and that through you, all things are possible. You will not let me despair, even when I am struck down; I am not destroyed, for that is not what you have in mind for me. My Protector, thank you for being a buffer for me when times are difficult.

All of us suffer through terrible things. How has God provided a buffer to protect you from the full brunt of a really tough time?

Helps/aids

God sees when we need help. When we are weak, he gives us strength; when we are in danger, he rescues us; when we are hurting, he heals us; when we are lacking something important, he renders the right kind of assistance. His aid transforms us from disadvantaged to favored.

> God is our refuge and strength, a very present help in trouble.
> —Psalm 46:1, ESV

> For I, the LORD your God, hold your right hand; it is I who say to you, "Fear not, I am the one who helps you."
> —Isaiah 41:13, ESV

My prayer: Lord, I have experienced your help in time of need. I am emboldened to ask you for aid in the tiniest things. You smile on me, and you help me. Thank you for caring about even the little things. It shows me that I must be bold and ask for your help in the big things, too. For then, your power will be seen and experienced by many, and you will be glorified.

When have you recently asked for God's help for something large or small? How did he come through and assist you?

Blinds

People can be spiritually blind and not recognize it until later. They are deprived of right judgment or reason. If our hearts are not right, God can prevent us from seeing. The Bible's book of Acts tells us that God temporarily blinded Saul of Tarsus so that Saul could see the truth of his actions, that in breathing out murderous threats toward Christians, he was persecuting Christ himself. Saul's temporary blindness was a key pivot point in the spread of Christianity.

> Be stunned and amazed, blind yourselves and be sightless;
> be drunk, but not from wine, stagger, but not from beer. The
> LORD has brought over you a deep sleep: He has sealed your
> eyes (the prophets); he has covered your heads (the seers).
> —Isaiah 29:9–10

> . . . as it is written: "God gave them a spirit of stupor, eyes that
> could not see and ears that could not hear, to this very day."
> —Romans 11:8

My prayer: Lord, some people whom I love are suffering from the curse of spiritual blindness. I pray that you will be merciful to them, as you were to me when I was blinded by the ways of the world. Please remove their blindness so that they too can see your unfailing love and grasp your outstretched hand.

Do you know someone who is spiritually blind? How can you address this spiritual state?

Permeates

In heaven and throughout the earth, God is present everywhere. More important, his love extends infinitely and pervades hearts and minds. When we invite him into our lives, he completely renews us, so that we can begin to see and live according to our true identity in Christ.

> Where can I go from Your Spirit? Or where can I flee from Your presence? If I ascend to heaven, You are there; if I make my bed in Sheol, behold, You are there. If I take the wings of the dawn, if I dwell in the remotest part of the sea, Even there Your hand will lead me, And Your right hand will take hold of me. —Psalm 139:7–10, NASB 2020

> Though they dig down to the depths below, from there my hand will take them. Though they climb up to the heavens above, from there I will bring them down. —Amos 9:2

My prayer: Lord, of course you permeate all things, all places secret or public. You made all of it, and you remain present. You are with me, my Lord and my God. Your Holy Spirit has lovingly pervaded my entire being. I praise you for never leaving me; as you have promised, you are always with me.

How does it feel to know that God permeates everything in your world, in your being?

Remembers

When we are in relationship with God, we never have to feel abandoned or forgotten by him. He always keeps us in mind. Actually, the word *remember* (*zakar* in Hebrew) goes beyond not forgetting; it indicates action. Through good times and bad, he not only remains aware of us, he takes action as he cares for us. With his great and perfect plan, he bears us in mind, rewarding us freely.

> But God remembered Noah and all the wild animals and the livestock that were with him in the ark, and he sent a wind over the earth, and the waters receded. —Genesis 8:1

> For he remembered his holy promise given to his servant Abraham. —Psalm 105:42

> God heard their groaning, and he remembered his covenant promise to Abraham, Isaac, and Jacob. —Exodus 2:24, NLT

My prayer: Lord, I love that your Scriptures document how you remember your people. Now, I am one of your people. You do remember me now and will in the future because you keep your promises, and you are unchanging. And you are always acting for my good. I pray that I, in turn, will remember to rely on your strength and your grace, giving thanks to you always.

In what ways has God remembered you by actively caring for you and rewarding you?

Shows/displays

Through acts of deliverance, mercy, and kindness, God allows us to see or perceive his power, goodness, faithfulness, and many other characteristics. He does this to guide us, to assure us, and to prove that he is who he says he is.

> Let the morning bring me word of your unfailing love, for I have put my trust in you. Show me the way I should go, for to you I entrust my life. —Psalm 143:8

> Summon your might, O God. Display your power, O God, as you have in the past. —Psalm 68:28, NLT

> "All the people of the land will bury them, and the day I display my glory will be a memorable day for them," declares the Sovereign LORD. —Ezekiel 39:13

My prayer: O Sovereign Lord, thank you for showing your strength, your love, your mercy to me. You are so holy, and therefore you could remain far away. You lovingly choose, instead, to draw me close to you as you display the goodness of your character.

In what ways has God displayed himself and his character to you?

Unerring/infallible

As humans, we find it difficult to imagine anyone being incapable of making mistakes or being wrong. But God is all-wise and perfect in every aspect. He is truth. It is impossible for him to lie, and we can trust him completely.

> God's way is unerring; the LORD's promise is refined; he is a
> shield for all who take refuge in him. —Psalm 18:31, NABRE

> He is the Rock, his works are perfect, and all his ways are just.
> A faithful God who does no wrong, upright and just is he.
> —Deuteronomy 32:4

My prayer: Great God in heaven and on earth, because of the work of the Holy Spirit, I trusted in you before I knew that your word and your way are infallible. I was willing to submit to you in faith. And now that I know you and your word better, I am confident that everything you say is true, and I can depend on your truth and justice. Thank you, my Rock, for this great assurance.

In what areas are you fallible? How do you address these faults with the Lord?

Resplendent

Even without seeing him face-to-face, we surely know that God is supremely impressive and attractive. When we see him in heaven, he will be dazzlingly sumptuous in beauty and majesty; in a word, breathtaking.

> You are resplendent and majestic coming down from the mountains of prey. —Psalm 76:4, HCSB

> Splendor and majesty are before him; strength and glory are in his sanctuary. —Psalm 96:6

> Praise the LORD, my soul. LORD my God, you are very great; you are clothed with splendor and majesty. —Psalm 104:1

My prayer: O holy God, I am awestruck, even tearful, at the thought of seeing you in all your glory, seated on high, in splendor and majesty, resplendent in the beauty of your heavens. Thank you for the way you have pictured yourself in the Bible and for giving me the certain hope of seeing you on your throne.

What or who in our world could be described as resplendent? What do you think will be your reaction when you see the Lord seated on his throne?

Exalted

Certainly no thing should be considered to be more important than God. There is no one who is above God. He is the most highly regarded being ever. We exalt him—we worship him—because of who he is and what he has done. He is deserving of our focus, our adoration, and all of our praise.

> He says, "Be still, and know that I am God; I will be exalted among the nations, I will be exalted in the earth."
> —Psalm 46:10

> In the year that King Uzziah died, I saw the Lord, high and exalted, seated on a throne; and the train of his robe filled the temple. —Isaiah 6:1

> Be exalted, O God, above the highest heavens. May your glory shine over all the earth. —Psalm 57:11, NLT

My prayer: Lord, you are so far above anything I can imagine. I have delved into your word to learn about you and draw close to you. I will continue to do so because I love you. The more I know, the less I can fathom your extreme and ultimate greatness in every aspect. And the more I know, the deeper my love for you grows.

Is there anything on earth that you praise and almost worship? If so, should you reconsider exalting these things?

Vast

Everything about God is vast; he is infinite in extent, depth, and intensity. All of this is impossible for humans to comprehend, for we are intellectually able to gauge things in only a few dimensions. But God does not fit into measurable dimensions nor into human constructs. His love, power, wisdom, righteousness, and creativity know no bounds.

> How precious to me are your thoughts, God! How vast is the sum of them! —Psalm 139:17

> His wisdom is profound, his power is vast. Who has resisted him and come out unscathed? —Job 9:4

My prayer: Thank you, O Lord, for including in your word so many examples of the vastness of your love and power, your creativity and righteousness. The sacrifice of your Son demonstrates how vast is your love for me! While I cannot comprehend how wide and long, high and deep is that love (Ephesians 3:18), I can devote myself to praising you.

When were you wowed by seeing something that seemed to be vast?

Supernatural

Beginning with creation—maybe even before—God has performed wonders that would be deemed impossible according to scientific understanding or the laws of nature. We must recognize that we are not talking about a force or a being who conforms to human norms or rules, and it is impossible to underestimate what God can and will do.

> He performs wonders that cannot be fathomed, miracles that cannot be counted. —Job 5:9

> This also comes from the LORD who commands armies, who gives supernatural guidance and imparts great wisdom. —Isaiah 28:29, NET

> Jesus looked at them and said, "With man this is impossible, but with God all things are possible." —Matthew 19:26

My prayer: Yes, Lord, you are beyond nature, for you created it. You are not just a force, you are *the* force of life, of everything that exists. I thank you for the many supernatural acts you have performed in my life, the foremost of which is the transformation of my heart. No one but you could have accomplished that. I am committed to honoring and praising you for your supernatural work.

Describe something that was seemingly impossible—even supernatural—that happened to you. How do you think it occurred?

Great

The word "great" is overused. People, events, or things are called great when we consider a particular ability or dimension: a great golfer, musician, scientist, or strategist. Frequently, we toss off, "Have a great day!" In contrast, God's greatness in every dimension, in every facet of his character and being, is immeasurable.

> For the LORD is the great God, the great King above all gods.
> —Psalm 95:3

> Great is the LORD and greatly to be praised in the city of our God! His holy mountain, beautiful in elevation, is the joy of all the earth, Mount Zion, in the far north, the city of the great King. —Psalm 48:1–2, ESV

My prayer: My Lord, you are great, immeasurably powerful, wise, merciful, and loving. I praise you because you are deserving of all praise. I love you because you first loved me. In your love and mercy, you have designed a blessed future for me. Thank you, my great, great God.

In what ways do you overuse or misuse the word "great"? What words could you use instead?

Rich

God is not only impressively magnificent, surpassing anything that we can imagine, he is rich—abundant—in every way. To our extreme fortune, he has invited us to be a part of his kingdom.

> Tear your hearts, not just your clothes, and return to the LORD your God. For he is gracious and compassionate, slow to anger, rich in faithful love, and he relents from sending disaster.
> —Joel 2:13, HCSB

> But because of his great love for us, God, who is rich in mercy, made us alive with Christ even when we were dead in transgressions—it is by grace you have been saved.
> —Ephesians 2:4–5

My prayer: Unbounded Lord, I have seen in my own life that you are rich in love, rich in mercy, rich in every good thing. You have showered me with an abundance of your patience, kindness, and love. Thank you for your compassion and for the promise of eternity with you.

Think about a rich experience you had. It might have been outwardly rich or inwardly rich. What was it about that experience that made it seem rich?

Wonderful/wondrous

By the wondrous, marvelous things he does, God inspires delight and admiration. We need only open our eyes to see and open our minds and hearts to appreciate the wonders he has for us.

> For to us a child is born, to us a son is given; and the government shall be upon his shoulder, and his name shall be called Wonderful Counselor, Mighty God, Everlasting Father, Prince of Peace. —Isaiah 9:6, ESV

> God thunders wondrously with his voice; he does great things that we cannot comprehend. —Job 37:5, ESV

My prayer: Awesome God, everything about you is too wonderful for words: your law, your works, your love, your grace. Your plan for my salvation, and for the salvation of many, is wonderful, breathtaking, seemingly too good to be true. Gratefully, I know that it is true. I marvel at every aspect of you, and I praise you and desire to know you more and more.

What are some of the wonders you have experienced?

Maker

God has beautifully and perfectly made all things. There is nothing that exists that did not begin with something that God made. And, incomprehensibly to us, he made—and continues to make—all things work together.

> As you do not know the path of the wind, or how the body
> is formed in a mother's womb, so you cannot understand the
> work of God, the Maker of all things. —Ecclesiastes 11:5

> How many are your works, LORD! In wisdom you made them
> all; the earth is full of your creatures. —Psalm 104:24

My prayer: In your great wisdom, O Lord, you made all things. You made all systems in the universe work together, systems that are so complex in their interconnectedness and interdependencies. You, my Lord, made them all, and in you they all hold together. I am so thankful to be connected to you and dependent on you for my physical, emotional, and spiritual wellbeing.

Consider the special care you took when you have made something. What have you handcrafted for someone else, and how was it received?

Measures

God measured each and every aspect of creation, above, in, and under the earth. He ascertained the required size and duration of each aspect, establishing weights and volumes, setting boundaries and time limits, so that all things would work together.

> Who has measured the waters in the hollow of his hand, or with the breadth of his hand marked off the heavens? Who has held the dust of the earth in a basket, or weighed the mountains on the scales and the hills in a balance? —Isaiah 40:12

> I will make justice the measuring line and righteousness the level; then hail will sweep away the refuge of lies, and the waters will overflow the secret place. —Isaiah 28:17, NASB 2020

My prayer: Lord, you alone knew how to set the dimensions for everything you have made, from things infinitely smaller than DNA to the whole cosmos. While I cannot comprehend even a tiny bit of the exactness required for the cohesion of the entire universe, I know that you made all of it with precision and wisdom and perfection.

You have been measured and equipped to fulfill the assignment that has been placed before you. What else, if anything, do you need in order to take on the challenge?

Fills

In creation, God filled the heavens and the earth. And he fills up each one of us; in him, we can be completely satisfied or even have more than enough. Because of his love for us, we can be filled with joy, understanding, conviction, wisdom, and peace.

> See, I have chosen Bezalel son of Uri, the son of Hur, of the tribe of Judah, and I have filled him with the Spirit of God, with wisdom, with understanding, with knowledge and with all kinds of skills. —Exodus 31:2–3

> This is what the LORD Almighty says: "In a little while I will once more shake the heavens and the earth, the sea and the dry land. I will shake all nations, and what is desired by all nations will come, and I will fill this house with glory," says the LORD Almighty. —Haggai 2:6–7

My prayer: God Almighty, I am awed when I think of your totality. When you fill me with joy, I am filled to overflowing. I know that when you filled me with the Holy Spirit, you did that completely. I praise you for your power, your love. Oh, how you fill me with every good thing!

People can be filled with many things: joy, understanding, conviction, wisdom, peace, or something else. In what way have you been filled?

Gives birth

Even though we are children of God, we don't think of God as *bearing* offspring. Yet, one of his Hebrew names, *El Chuwl*, means The God Who Gave Birth or The God Who Gave You Life. He is the one who gives us life when we are born. When we are reborn, he seals us by giving us the Holy Spirit, guaranteeing our redemption.

> Before the mountains were born, before you gave birth to the earth and the world, from beginning to end, you are God.
> —Psalm 90:2, NLT

> For everyone who has been born of God overcomes the world. And this is the victory that has overcome the world—our faith.
> —1 John 5:4, ESV

> You deserted the Rock, who fathered you; you forgot the God who gave you birth. —Deuteronomy 32:18

My prayer: Lord, you gave birth to everything and, of greatest importance, you brought about human life for your Son. Thank you for my first birth and for my rebirth. Through my rebirth, you brought me into your family and gave me the opportunity to have a grace-filled life here on earth, then eternal life, with you. I will not forget to praise you for your goodness.

What was remarkable about your initial birth or about your rebirth?

Enables/empowers

God provides the means, the strength, the way, to do what we need to do. When we ask him, he helps us see more clearly, listen more attentively, and act more effectively. He is Almighty God, and he willingly shares some of his power with us to help us accomplish his will.

> The fear of the LORD is a fountain of life, enabling anyone to escape the snares of death. —Proverbs 14:27, ISV
>
> But you will receive power when the Holy Spirit has come upon you, and you will be my witnesses in Jerusalem and in all Judea and Samaria, and to the end of the earth. —Acts 1:8, ESV
>
> . . . and there are varieties of activities, but it is the same God who empowers them all in everyone. —1 Corinthians 12:6, ESV

My prayer: Almighty God, you have enabled me to love and follow you by laying out before me everything that I need, lifting up my Lord Jesus Christ so that I can see him daily, moment by moment. Thank you for choosing me, for loving me, for giving me the means to see how you were working even before I came to love you, and thank you for empowering me to do your will.

What have you been empowered to do?

Unconditionally loves

God is perfect in everything he does, including the way he loves us. His love is without limitations. He loves us no matter what happens. What a different world it would be if everyone would or could love unconditionally.

> But God demonstrates his own love for us in this: while we were still sinners, Christ died for us. —Romans 5:8

> For I am convinced that neither death nor life, neither angels nor demons, neither the present nor the future, nor any powers, neither height nor depth, nor anything else in all creation, will be able to separate us from the love of God that is in Christ Jesus our Lord. —Romans 8:38–39

My prayer: Father, so much—maybe everything—in this world is conditional. It is hard, so hard, to imagine that you can—and do—love me in spite of everything I have done in the past, my current sinful thoughts, and the repugnant things that I will inevitably do. But these things I know: you love me, and nothing will stand in the way of your love. I love you and want to please you, not to win your love, for I know that I am covered by your love into eternity.

How would this world be different if everyone loved unconditionally?

Approachable

One of the many mysteries about God is that, as holy as he is, he is approachable, easy to talk to. He invites us to be with him. We have immediate access to him. He doesn't block us from coming to him; there's no special method of communicating with him. We can just talk. He is willing to listen.

> Then Jesus said, "Leave the children alone, and don't try to keep them from coming to Me, because the kingdom of heaven is made up of people like this." —Matthew 19:14, HCSB

> A bruised reed he will not break, and a smoldering wick he will not snuff out, till he has brought justice through to victory. —Matthew 12:20

> Let us then approach God's throne of grace with confidence, so that we may receive mercy and find grace to help us in our time of need. —Hebrews 4:16

My prayer: My Lord and Savior, I was so vulnerable, so lost in sin, a bruised reed, smoldering and worthy of being snuffed out entirely. But you rescued me by removing the scales from my eyes. You showed me that you are approachable, and you proved that you desire me to be in your holy presence. Thank you for your dizzying grace and unfathomable love.

What makes a person approachable? How do you express your approachability?

Listens

God doesn't just hear us, he listens to the heart of what we say to him. He understands that what we bring to him is serious, important, and true. He lovingly wants to hear from us.

> If I had not confessed the sin in my heart, the Lord would not have listened. But God did listen! He paid attention to my prayer. —Psalm 66:18–19, NLT

> We know that God does not listen to [unrepentant] sinners. He listens to the godly person who does his will. —John 9:31

My prayer: Lord, although you command me to be holy as you are holy, I am not holy; I am not righteous; I abhor my sins. I cherish the fact that you listen to me—and you do it perfectly because you know my heart. Thank you for always being with me and for truly caring about my concerns.

Who in your life listened, really listened, to you? How did you know they were listening to your heart?

Bears

God bears our burdens. He supports the heavy weight that we carry. It helps to know that he cares and is willing and able to alleviate some of the stress—or free us altogether—of those burdens.

> Praise be to the Lord, to God our Savior, who daily bears our burdens. —Psalm 68:19

> Give your burdens to the LORD, and he will take care of you. He will not permit the godly to slip and fall. —Psalm 55:22, NLT

My prayer: Merciful Father, thank you for bearing so much for me. You have told me to leave my burdens with you, so that I do not have to carry them. You want me to be free to love and serve you without being weighed down by doubts and painful memories of wrongs and missteps. Thank you for bearing my burdens for me and for bearing with me.

Who has carried some of your burdens? In what way did they do that? For whom have you stepped up to shoulder some of the weight they had been carrying?

Assures

It is comforting to have someone confidently dispel doubts or make certain that something will—or won't—happen. God gives us the confidence that he has every situation under his control, no matter how difficult it may seem.

> And the work of righteousness shall be peace; and the effect of righteousness quietness and assurance forever.
> —Isaiah 32:17, KJ2000

> Let us draw near to God with a sincere heart and with the full assurance that faith brings, having our hearts sprinkled to cleanse us from a guilty conscience and having our bodies washed with pure water. —Hebrews 10:22

My prayer: Lord God, you have proven completely faithful throughout time, and this assures me that I can have full confidence in you, going forward. I am at peace knowing that all of your promises are true. Your loving words and mighty acts remove my doubts and cradle me in assurance.

Who provided assurance to you when you were in a difficult situation? How did they do that?

Refuge/shelter

God provides a sure place of refuge in times of trouble. He is a retreat, even an oasis, for us when we need refreshment. And he is a sanctuary, a safe harbor, when we are in need of protection.

> You have been a refuge for the poor, a refuge for the needy
> in their distress, a shelter from the storm and a shade from
> the heat. For the breath of the ruthless is like a storm driving
> against a wall. —Isaiah 25:4

> I will say of the LORD, "He is my refuge and my fortress, my
> God, in whom I trust." —Psalm 91:2

My prayer: Lord, I abide in you and you in me. You not only provide a refuge, you *are* the refuge, my haven, my astonishingly beautiful "best place" to be. Thank you for your tender care and for the peace that I have under your protective wing.

How would you describe your favorite place of refuge or sanctuary? And why does it provide emotional, spiritual, or physical shelter for you?

Brings

If we are willing to believe and receive, God ushers us into a place of peace, joy, and hope. All of this gracious goodness comes to us as a result of God's first bringing his Son, Jesus Christ, into our broken world to save us from the just penalty for our sins. We need only to receive the extraordinary gift of salvation by trusting in him.

> It was the LORD our God himself who brought us and our parents up out of Egypt, from that land of slavery, and performed those great signs before our eyes. He protected us on our entire journey and among all the nations through which we traveled. —Joshua 24:17

> From this man's descendants God has brought to Israel the Savior Jesus, as he promised. —Acts 13:23

My prayer: Lord, you have brought me out of sin's enslavement into a place of safety, joy, peace, and resurrection power. Help me to recognize and tap into your power to bring others to the feet of Jesus, so that you can bring those same treasures into their lives.

What person, event, or idea has God brought into your life that made a significant shift in your thinking or behavior?

Relieves

We live in a broken world, so we have pain, distress, and difficulty in our lives. Because he loves us, God often causes those hardships to become less severe or serious. He is able to help us with anything. Nothing is too difficult for him.

> Come to me, all you who are weary and burdened, and I will give you rest. —Matthew 11:28

> He will wipe every tear from their eyes. There will be no more death or mourning or crying or pain, for the old order of things has passed away. —Revelation 21:4

My prayer: Lord, I know that I can bring anything before you—any distress or adversity—and you are able to relieve it. After all, you made the entire universe. And you love me, so if it fits within your perfect will, you will relieve the difficulty. If I am willing to give my anxiety to you, you will give me peace. Such a blessing!

In what ways have pain, distress, or difficulties in your life been relieved?

Searches/probes

Nothing is hidden from God. He thoroughly probes our minds and hearts, and he knows our inmost secrets. We do set up defensive barriers in order to protect the hard, hurt places, but he knows how to dissolve those barriers. As he does so, God offers the joy of healing.

> For the Lord GOD says this: "Behold, I Myself will search for
> My sheep and look after them. As a shepherd cares for his flock
> on a day when he is among his scattered sheep, so I will care
> for My sheep and will rescue them from all the places where
> they were scattered on a cloudy and gloomy day."
> —Ezekiel 34:11–12, NASB 2020

> And I know, God, that it is you who searches the heart and you
> who finds pleasure in righteousness. With a righteous heart
> I have freely given all these things, and now I have seen all of
> these people of yours giving freely and joyfully to you!
> —1 Chronicles 29:17, ISV

My prayer: Holy and loving God, you sought me out as a sheep that was precious to you. And you have searched my heart and mind. Thank you for showing me what is offensive in your sight. Please give me strength to increase in righteousness; it is my heart's desire to please you.

Inviting God to examine your motives and secret thoughts brings you to a place of confession and healing. What was the last time you searched your own heart and invited God to do so as well?

Judges

God's nature is one of perfect justice because he is perfectly righteous. He judges everyone with perfect equity and rewards us according to our works. He knows what we have done as well as who and what we are deep down inside.

> It is God who judges: He brings one down, he exalts another.
> —Psalm 75:7

> He will not judge by what he sees with his eyes, or decide by what he hears with his ears; but with righteousness he will judge the needy, with justice he will give decisions for the poor of the earth. He will strike the earth with the rod of his mouth; with the breath of his lips he will slay the wicked.
> —Isaiah 11:3b–4

> That's the whole story. Here now is my final conclusion: Fear God and obey his commands, for this is everyone's duty. God will judge us for everything we do, including every secret thing, whether good or bad. —Ecclesiastes 12:13–14, NLT

My prayer: You, Lord, are the only one who can judge rightly. You see within me and judge my heart and my intentions. Thank you for seeing me through the righteousness of Jesus Christ, whose blood cleanses me from all unrighteousness.

Most people dislike being judged. How do you feel about God judging you, your heart, and your intentions?

Hardens

Indeed, God judges us by what is in our hearts. He completely knows the status of our faith and our future willingness to believe his truth. Accordingly, he decides, at some point, to make our hearts become harder and more severe, or he opts to make them softer and more sympathetic.

> Then the LORD said to Moses, "Go to Pharaoh, for I have hardened his heart and the hearts of his officials so that I may perform these signs of mine among them." —Exodus 10:1

> Therefore God has mercy on whom he wants to have mercy, and he hardens whom he wants to harden. —Romans 9:18

My prayer: Forgiving God, I cry out to you that you will soften, and have not hardened, the hearts of some of my loved ones. I am concerned that they may be wandering. As they stray, there is grave danger that their hearts will become hardened. The desire of my heart, which you truly know, is that they will not miss the opportunity to come to know you.

What can you do to reach people whose hearts are in danger of being forever hardened?

Requires

As we consider what God has done for us, it is good to know what God requires of us. Given the scale of his provisions for us—now and eternally—we should do our very best to meet our obligation to honor him.

> And now, Israel, what does the LORD your God require of you? He requires only that you fear the LORD your God, and live in a way that pleases him, and love him and serve him with all your heart and soul. And you must always obey the LORD's commands and decrees that I am giving you today for your own good. —Deuteronomy 10:12–13, NLT

> He has shown you, O mortal, what is good. And what does the LORD require of you? To act justly and to love mercy and to walk humbly with your God. —Micah 6:8

My prayer: Gracious Lord, we humans often look to do only what is required. Nothing more. While your requirements are challenging, they are for our own good, to help us in our daily lives. Our obligation becomes joy as we draw near you and please you!

How do you think you have measured up this past week in terms of being just, loving, and humble?

Clears the way / removes barriers

God is with us; God is for us; God has a plan for us. He knows what lies ahead, and he removes obstacles that stand in the way of our progress. He has made it clear that he *will* achieve his purpose.

> I will go before you and will level the mountains; I will break
> down gates of bronze and cut through bars of iron.
> —Isaiah 45:2

> Now may our God and Father himself and our Lord Jesus clear
> the way for us to come to you. —1 Thessalonians 3:11

My prayer: O Lord, my God, I have made my own way difficult. But now through your grace, I have learned to call on you, and you help me. Thank you for clearing the way for me through Christ Jesus and for removing barriers day by day, especially those that block a deeper relationship with you.

What barriers are blocking, even partially, a deeper relationship with God?

Veils

God is always watching out for us. He knows what is best for us. He knows we cannot handle a full view of the future, so God lovingly veils it from us. Similarly, we cannot endure a complete exposure to his glory, so (in Jesus) he veiled himself in flesh when he came to show us the way to live on earth and be with him forever.

> He shrouded himself in darkness, veiling his approach with dense rain clouds. —2 Samuel 22:12, NLT

> He has blocked my way so that I cannot pass through; He has veiled my paths with darkness. —Job 19:8, HCSB

My prayer: My Lord, I am so thankful that you do veil your approach. You reveal just the right amount of yourself to me, because I would be stunned, knocked down, by the full impact of your holiness. Thank you for coming to earth and for veiling the deity of Jesus. Although some refused to see, he showed all people at least some of who you are. Humanity could not bear to see and experience the fullness of you, but you were glorified through your Son, and he—veiled in flesh—modeled in human terms what it looks like to be like you.

What has happened to you that, in retrospect, you are glad you did not see coming?

Teaches

Through the Bible, God instructs us in the way we should live. He has imparted knowledge and insights to many, many people throughout the centuries—and does so even today. And he sent the greatest teacher, Jesus, to illuminate our minds and hearts and to show us how to love God and one another.

> Who, then, are those who fear the LORD? He will instruct them in the way they should choose. —Psalm 25:12

> Now go; I will help you speak and will teach you what to say. —Exodus 4:12

> Behold, you delight in truth in the inward being, and you teach me wisdom in the secret heart. —Psalm 51:6, ESV

My prayer: Wise and loving Lord, you have taught me for many years and continue to teach me. Thank you for your gentle and consistent instruction. Thank you for loving me so much that you do not allow me to remain in ignorance. I pray that you will continue to open my eyes, ears, and heart to your instruction.

Who was your best teacher ever? What was it about them or their approach that made them effective in teaching you?

Clarifies

God works in many ways so that he can be clearly seen and his message can be completely understood. Further, God makes our out-of-sync position clear to us. He shows us our foolishness, our waywardness. Our first reaction might be shame or denial, but he brings the truth to light so that, if we are willing, we can understand and benefit.

> For since the creation of the world God's invisible qualities—
> his eternal power and divine nature—have been clearly seen,
> being understood from what has been made, so that people are
> without excuse. —Romans 1:20

> All of us, then, who are mature should take such a view of
> things. And if on some point you think differently, that too
> God will make clear to you. —Philippians 3:15

My prayer: Father, Creator, you have made it clear to me that you love me. You gave your Son to me to save me. You've made your message perfectly clear. Thank you for that message, for your gifts, especially for the gift of eternal life that you offer to everyone, if each one will only hear your clarion call.

What about God has become more clear to you during the past year? And how has that come about?

Tramples

Because he wants what is best for us, God warns that he can and will tread on, crush, trample us if we are not in his will at the time of final judgment. Some people refuse to believe that a loving God would do this, but they would be wise to acknowledge who he is and pay him due respect.

> In indignation you marched through the earth; In anger you trampled the nations. You went forth for the salvation of your people, for the salvation of your anointed. You smashed the head of the house of evil To uncover him from foot to neck. *Selah.* —Habakkuk 3:12–13, NASB 2020

> I have trodden the winepress alone; from the nations no one was with me. I trampled them in my anger and trod them down in my wrath; their blood spattered my garments, and I stained all my clothing. —Isaiah 63:3

My prayer: My great Lord, some will refuse your call and choose the supposed deliciousness of sin. I envision a picture of sin blooming in earth's great vineyard, growing into plump, tantalizing, but bitter fruit. But the earth is your vineyard. I know you will ultimately crush sin. Final judgment will be a horror for those who are not yours. I am so grateful that your goodness and your justice demand that you trample sin. Thank you for viewing me through the righteousness of your beloved, sinless Son, so that I will be saved from your wrath in the last days.

What sin of yours are you actually happy that God has trampled on?

Restores

Our loving God is willing to reinstate good things that have somehow been lost. He brings back health and relationships; he revives our spirit when we are exhausted or anxious.

> He restores my soul; he guides me in the paths of righteousness for the sake of his name. —Psalm 23:3, NASB 2020

> He will pray to God, and God will delight in him. That man will see his face with a shout of joy, and God will restore his righteousness to him. —Job 33:26, HCSB

> For the LORD will restore the splendor of Jacob like the splendor of Israel. —Nahum 2:2a, NASB 2020

My prayer: Lord, you have a vision for the way things could be: perfect and beautiful, loving and righteous. Too often I fall short of your best for me. So, you have made a way. You restore me daily, hourly, and minute by minute. Thank you this restoration. Help me, I pray, to keep to the right path in all of my relationships.

How has your spirit been restored when you have been exhausted or anxious? What is your part in bringing back health in relationships that are hurting?

Majestic

When we try to picture God, we think of him as having glorious splendor, extraordinary majesty, and lofty dignity. And, given everything we know about him, these descriptions must be only the beginning. We are limited in our ability to adequately put into words what God must be like, but oh, how majestic he must be.

> Out of the north he comes in golden splendor; God comes in awesome majesty. —Job 37:22
>
> Honor and majesty surround him; strength and joy fill his dwelling. —1 Chronicles 16:27, NLT
>
> They will speak of the glorious splendor of your majesty—and I will meditate on your wonderful works. —Psalm 145:5

My prayer: Lord God Almighty, it is a marvel that you, who are infinitely lofty, would call me into relationship with you. It may be that our sweet relationship causes me to err in being too familiar with the King, the Creator of the universe, but in my heart, you are my Abba. In contrast to our close relationship here on earth, I am certain that when I see you on your incredible throne, I will fall at your feet in worship. Even before seeing you in heaven, I know that you are too majestic for words.

When you meditate on God's majesty, what imagery comes to mind?

High and lifted up

God is lofty, both in character and spirit. He is supremely noble and superior to everything and everyone. His sovereignty is complete, and he is high above all. We cannot add to his glory. Rather, when we "lift him up," we acknowledge—in our hearts and before men—that our own sinful actions have brought shame to his name, and we praise him as we recognize his rightful place.

> For this is what the high and exalted One says—he who lives forever, whose name is holy: "I live in a high and holy place, but also with the one who is contrite and lowly in spirit, to revive the spirit of the lowly and to revive the heart of the contrite." —Isaiah 57:15

> But who is able to build a temple for him, since the heavens, even the highest heavens, cannot contain him? Who then am I to build a temple for him, except as a place to burn sacrifices before him? —2 Chronicles 2:6

My prayer: Lord of lords, King of kings, you are high and above all things. Inexplicably, despite the fact that you are impressively superior, many cannot (or will not) see you in that way. I pray that you will show me how I can be your instrument in helping others see that your name, and your Son, are high and lifted up above all things, deserving of all praise.

In what ways do you acknowledge God's rightful, exalted place?

The standard

God is the standard by which all things are measured. He has perfect love, perfect mercy, perfect justice, perfect holiness, and he is perfect in every way. When he came to earth as a human, Jesus showed us what that standard looks like.

> So you must keep his commandments, live according to his standards, and revere him. —Deuteronomy 8:6, NET

> [God said to Moses,] "Speak to the entire assembly of Israel and say to them: 'Be holy because I, the LORD your God, am holy.'" —Leviticus 19:2

> For I have given you an example, that you also should do just as I have done to you. —John 13:15, ESV

My prayer: Lord, your standard is perfection. In Matthew 5:48, I am commanded to be perfect as you are perfect. Without the saving work of Jesus, I am not even headed in the right direction. Here on earth, by the power of the Holy Spirit, I can be obedient and responsive to your transforming hand. Thank you for helping me to conform more and more to your standard, for I know it is your best for me.

What is one way God is helping you change so that you can conform to a higher standard, one that looks more like Jesus?

Truth

God expresses his being and character in truth. In the Gospel according to John, Jesus says he is the way, the truth, and the life. Jesus is the only way for us to be acceptable in God's presence; he is the truth because he is the perfect revelation of the Father, and he is the life because through him we have eternal life.

> Guide me in your truth and teach me, for you are God my Savior, and my hope is in you all day long. —Psalm 25:5

> Into your hands I commit my spirit; for you have redeemed me, LORD God of truth. —Psalm 31:5, ISV

My prayer: Lord, you have shown me that Jesus is the way, the truth, and the life. Your word proves, time and again, that all truth resides in you. Satan works hard to distort the truth. But, because you are truth, you can never lie, and you will never fail me. Please guide my steps, so that my actions will not deny the truth of who you are.

What truth(s) have been most impactful in refining your understanding of the way God has been working in your life?

All-sufficient

God's name, *El Shaddai*, means God Almighty, The All-Sufficient One, The God Who Is More Than Enough. God is infinitely able to provide for himself and doesn't depend on us to supply anything for him. Still, he desires relationship with us.

> If I were hungry I would not tell you, for the world is mine, and all that is in it. —Psalm 50:12

> The God who made the world and everything in it is the Lord of heaven and earth and does not live in temples built by human hands. And he is not served by human hands, as if he needed anything. Rather, he himself gives everyone life and breath and everything else. —Acts 17:24–25

My prayer: Lord, you don't need me as an agent to help complete your plans, for you will achieve your purpose no matter what. But you chose me to do my part. You love me, and you do have a purpose for me. I am so thankful that, although your plan will be accomplished with or without my service, you have made a place for me in your plan.

In what ways is it encouraging to know that God is all-sufficient and does not need anything?

Genuine/real

God is the real thing. He is authentic, not manufactured, not created, not fictitious. He is everything that he says he is, and he has proved himself to be faithful to his own description.

> You were shown these things so that you might know that the LORD is God; besides him there is no other. —Deuteronomy 4:35

> Then all the nations of the earth will recognize that the LORD is the only genuine God. —1 Kings 8:60, NET

My prayer: God of Truth, I know that you are genuine, real, authentic. There is no one like you. You are not a counterfeit god. Anyone—everyone—can recognize you by your wondrous works in creation and your supernatural involvement in the lives of real people, people like me. I pray that the fruit of your work in my life will display the reality of who you are and will draw others to you.

What was one important way in which God has proven himself to be real to you?

Deep/profound

Because of his infinite knowledge and wisdom, God's thoughts are profound, impossible for us to fully grasp. This is both reassuring and alluring. It comforts us to realize that he is such a great big God, and it invites us to learn more and more about him.

> These are the things God has revealed to us by his Spirit. The Spirit searches all things, even the deep things of God.
> —1 Corinthians 2:10

> They [God's mysteries and limits] are higher than the heavens above—what can you do? They are deeper than the depths below—what can you know? Their measure is longer than the earth and wider than the sea. —Job 11:8–9

My prayer: O God, it is impossible to describe the depth of your greatness, though many have tried. You are so profoundly holy, so loving, so faithful, so merciful, so *everything* that is good. Thank you for your Holy Spirit who communicates to my soul your love, power, and faithfulness, so that my soul can drink in even a small measure of who you are.

What is it about God that invites you to know him more deeply?

Stretches

When God stretches out his hand or arm, he leverages his infinite power. By this action, he made the heavens and conquered nations. In love, God stretches us to expand our knowledge and spiritual depth, so that we can draw closer to him.

> He made the earth by his power; he founded the world by his wisdom and stretched out the heavens by his understanding.
> —Jeremiah 51:15

> Remember today that your children were not the ones who saw and experienced the discipline of the LORD your God: his majesty, his mighty hand, his outstretched arm.
> —Deuteronomy 11:2

My prayer: Almighty God, the extent of your power and love is unspeakable, and I want to continually glorify you and all that you are. I am picturing your protective, outstretched arm above and around me. Thank you for the length, breadth, height, and depth of your love and for your wisdom in forming, guiding, and protecting me.

Over what circumstance in your own life today would you like to be assured of God's outstretched arm?

Commands

God has the utmost authority, and when he gives a command, we should do what he tells us to do. Being perfectly loving and good, he would never command us to do something that is not ultimately in our best interests. Although we do not always understand their reasons, his commands are for our good.

> Love the LORD your God and keep his requirements, his decrees, his laws and his commands always. —Deuteronomy 11:1

> The commandments of the LORD are right, bringing joy to the heart. The commands of the LORD are clear, giving insight for living. —Psalm 19:8, NLT

> And this is love: that we walk in obedience to his commands. As you have heard from the beginning, his command is that you walk in love. —2 John 1:6

My prayer: Lord, I know your commands, yet to my shame, I do not follow them fully. I do not honor you to the fullest; my efforts fall short. I do not love my neighbor and promote justice for the disadvantaged as thoroughly as I should. Please help me obey your commands, so that you can have your way with me in this world of sin.

Which of God's commands is the most difficult for you to obey?

Custom-maker

When something is made to particular requirements, it is special indeed. God has custom-built each of us to his own divine specifications, so that we fit perfectly into his overall plan.

> I praise you, for I am fearfully and wonderfully made. Wonderful are your works; my soul knows it very well.
> —Psalm 139:14, ESV

> For we are God's handiwork, created in Christ Jesus to do good works, which God prepared in advance for us to do.
> —Ephesians 2:10

My prayer: Lord, you crafted me in the way you thought was best, unique in all the world, just the way you wanted. You custom-made me for your good purposes. Thank you for opening my heart to respond to your call.

What handcrafted, custom-made thing has been special to you, and why?

Equips

God prepares us spiritually, emotionally, even physically, to do his work. He knows what we lack as well as when and how to augment our abilities. He supplies everything we need as we work to fulfill his purpose.

> May the God of peace . . . equip you with everything good for doing his will, and may he work in us what is pleasing to him, through Jesus Christ, to whom be glory for ever and ever. Amen. —Hebrews 13:20a–21

> All Scripture is God-breathed and is useful for teaching, rebuking, correcting, and training in righteousness, so that the servant of God may be thoroughly equipped for every good work. —2 Timothy 3:16–17

My prayer: Lord, the task of sufficiently representing you is impossible through my own resources, but you do equip me day by day, moment by moment, to face the challenge. When I fall short, the Holy Spirit helps me by cushioning the ears of the listener, so that they can hear your intentions, so that your good purposes can be achieved. It is not by my wisdom or knowledge, but only by your grace and equipping.

In what way(s) have you been equipped to do the work God has set out for you to do?

Awakens

Some people sleepwalk through life, quite unaware of God, his plan, and his saving grace. In love and to achieve his purpose, God rouses us from that sleep. Awakened by God, we understand that we have been missing his blessing, and it is time to get moving.

> The Lord GOD has given me the tongue of those who are taught, that I may know how to sustain with a word him who is weary. Morning by morning he awakens; he awakens my ear to hear as those who are taught. —Isaiah 50:4, ESV

> Remember, therefore, what you have received and heard; hold it fast, and repent. But if you do not wake up, I will come like a thief, and you will not know at what time I will come to you. —Revelation 3:3

My prayer: You well know, Lord God, that my "natural" self wants to just "go along" and enjoy a pleasant life. Dearest Lord, thank you for rousing me from my spiritual sleep, from sleepwalking through days and weeks without seeing, without knowing, without acknowledging the riches you provide. I want to rise and fully serve you, so that others can know and serve you too.

At some time you were awakened to realize that you had been missing a blessing. What was the time and the particular blessing?

Opens

God makes it possible for us to see, to hear, and to understand as he opens our eyes, our ears, and our hearts. He opens his kingdom to all who will seek him.

> Then God opened her eyes and she saw a well of water. So she went and filled the skin with water and gave the boy a drink.
> —Genesis 21:19

> The LORD opens the eyes of the blind. The LORD lifts up those who are weighed down. The LORD loves the godly.
> —Psalm 146:8, NLT

> And Elisha prayed, "O LORD, open his eyes so he may see." Then the LORD opened the servant's eyes and he saw that the hill was full of horses and chariots of fire all around Elisha.
> —2 Kings 6:17, NET

My prayer: Lord, you have opened my eyes to see the wonderful life that you have available to me. You have opened my ears to hear the truth of your word. You have opened my heart to receive your love and show your love to others. I praise you for all the ways in which you have opened the way for me to find you. Truly, you have opened heaven's gates for me.

Considering everything that has happened during the past year, to what opportunity, blessing, or circumstances have your eyes been opened?

Abides/dwells within

God is inherently present. He is always with us through his Holy Spirit. When we invite him to live in our hearts, he guides us along the right path, strengthens us to stand up to sin, teaches us what we need to know and do, and brings God's teachings to our remembrance.

> So we have come to know and to believe the love that God has for us. God is love, and whoever abides in love abides in God, and God abides in him. —1 John 4:16, ESV

> If you abide in me, and my words abide in you, ask whatever you wish, and it will be done for you. —John 15:7, ESV

My prayer: Lord, it gives me so much comfort to know that we are in permanent relationship; you dwell within my heart; you live in my mind. You bear with me and wait for me as I more closely align my thoughts and actions in accordance with your will for me.

Describe the difference between visiting a place and actually taking up residence. How have you made your heart a welcoming place for Holy Spirit to dwell?

Gathers

God brings together his people from various places, and what a joyful assembly that is. Each person in this gathering has a role in God's perfect plan for humankind.

> . . . but if you return to me and obey my commands, then even if your exiled people are at the farthest horizon, I will gather them from there and bring them to the place I have chosen as a dwelling for my Name. —Nehemiah 1:9

> The Sovereign LORD declares—he who gathers the exiles of Israel: "I will gather still others to them besides those already gathered." —Isaiah 56:8

My prayer: Loving Father, when you gather your people together here on earth, we are not strangers, for we have the same Father in heaven. We have a special kinship. I know that you will ultimately gather up all of your own and bring us into a beautiful eternity with you. In the meantime, Lord, thank you for protecting us under your wing. Thank you for the assurance that you have a place for me and consider me your own.

What do you find to be special about gathering with like-minded people, kindred spirits?

Protects

God shields us from harm. He guards us from above, behind, ahead, and on each side. He is right there, unfailing in his protection, especially from spiritual danger.

> O LORD, shelter me from the power of the wicked! Protect me
> from violent men, who plan to knock me over.
> —Psalm 140:4, NET

> "Because he loves me," says the LORD, "I will rescue him; I will
> protect him, for he acknowledges my name." —Psalm 91:14

My prayer: My Lord, I cannot even imagine how many times you have protected me from earthly dangers or from the evil one. I can single out certain times, of course, and I thank you for all of the times, known and unknown, when you have sustained me. You didn't let me fall. Thank you for your protection, for sheltering me.

Can you think of a time when you were protected from harm, including spiritual danger? What happened?

Cradles/rocks

Sometimes, like babies, we feel that it would be so good to be held gently and protectively, cradled and rocked. That is a luxury God provides to us, his precious ones. He holds us, comforts us, and helps us know that he is there for us.

> In peace I will lie down and sleep, for you alone, LORD, make me dwell in safety. —Psalm 4:8

> As a mother comforts her child, so will I comfort you; and you will be comforted over Jerusalem. —Isaiah 66:13

My prayer: Gentle Shepherd, when I am sleepless or afraid, you bend down and pick me up and cradle me in your strong arms. You whisper words of comfort that I need to hear. I praise you for keeping me in your tender, protective care whether I am awake or asleep.

When would you like God to cradle or rock you in his arms?

Nurtures

God cares for us in every way, giving us everything we need to grow toward him in deeper relationship. He encourages our spiritual development. He places us in situations in which we can receive training, learn discipline, and gain understanding, so that we can become mature in our walk with him.

> Listen, my sons, to a father's instruction; pay attention and gain understanding. I give you sound learning, so do not forsake my teaching. For I too was a son to my father, still tender, and cherished by my mother. Then he taught me, and he said to me, "Take hold of my words with all your heart; keep my commands, and you will live." —Proverbs 4:1–4

> For the Spirit God gave us does not make us timid, but gives us power, love and self-discipline. —2 Timothy 1:7

My prayer: Loving Father, thank you for nurturing me in your perfect way. You know all of my needs, for you truly see me. You provide everything I need. You encourage me, training me to grow in the way that is best. Again, thank you.

What are some ways in which God has nurtured you so that you could grow in relationship with him?

Counsels

If we ask for it, God gives us advice, telling us things we need to know. He provides insights into our own actions and those of others. He answers our questions, walks us through problems, and helps us in so many ways.

> I will instruct you and teach you in the way you should go; I will counsel you with my loving eye on you. —Psalm 32:8

> There are many plans in a person's mind, but it is the counsel of the LORD which will stand. —Proverbs 19:21, NET

> The counsel of the LORD stands forever, the plans of his heart to all generations. —Psalm 33:11, ESV

My prayer: Lord, I have seen in my own life that you do counsel me with a loving eye. You know what is best for me within your overall plan, and yet sometimes I do not listen. It seems I have my own plan. Please forgive me for my impatience or immediate selfishness. Help me to listen to your wise and loving counsel.

What advice would you like to ask of God for today or the coming week?

Reminds

Life is full of lessons. We have God's word to teach us what we need to know. The Holy Spirit helps us recall God's word in our day-to-day lives. If we don't remember its lessons, the Holy Spirit brings them to mind, so we can benefit from them.

> Remember the former things, those of long ago; I am God, and there is no other; I am God, and there is none like me.
> —Isaiah 46:9

> But the Advocate, the Holy Spirit, whom the Father will send in my name, will teach you all things and will remind you of everything I have said to you. —John 14:26

My prayer: Lord, I love that you are in my heart and in my mind and that you remind me of your promises. You prompt me to do what is right, and your Holy Spirit helps me to recall your word for my good. Thank you for your ever-presence and your love as you guide me in the ways that are best.

Contemplate and comment on how good it is to be reminded of something important.

Knows

God perceives everything; he is always able to discern fact from fiction. He knows us; he knows our hearts, our motivations, and our circumstances. Because he knows us so thoroughly, he knows when to discipline us, when to spur us on, and when to comfort us.

> Then hear from heaven, your dwelling place. Forgive and act;
> deal with everyone according to all they do, since you know
> their hearts (for you alone know every human heart).
> —1 Kings 8:39
>
> If our hearts condemn us, we know that God is greater than
> our hearts, and he knows everything. —1 John 3:20

My prayer: Lord of all, I love that you know everything about me in my past, present, and future. The fact that you know all of my faults and failures does not disturb me; instead, it gives me comfort that you really know me and still love me. Thank you for your invitation to know you ever more completely. It is quite wonderful to be growing, not just in "head knowledge," but "heart knowledge" as well.

In what way are you comforted by the fact that God thoroughly knows everything about you?

Testifies

God's word testifies of his plan for our salvation. The evidence he has given is exceptionally vast. His promises, documented in the Old Testament, all prove true, particularly through the ancestry, life, and ultimately the sacrifice of his Son, Jesus. That sacrifice results in our salvation when we believe.

> The Spirit himself testifies with our spirit that we are God's children. —Romans 8:16

> Since we believe human testimony, surely we can believe the greater testimony that comes from God. And God has testified about his Son. —1 John 5:9, NLT

> How shall we escape if we ignore so great a salvation? This salvation, which was first announced by the Lord, was confirmed to us by those who heard him. God also testified to it by signs, wonders and various miracles, and by gifts of the Holy Spirit distributed according to his will. —Hebrews 2:3–4

My prayer: Lord, you have proven your love, your faithfulness, your protection, your plan—all of it—in myriad ways. Thank you for confirming, proving, bearing witness, and testifying to me in so many different ways so that I may perceive your love and obey you.

What testimony of God has been significant in your life?

Reproaches/disapproves

God knows how to express his disapproval or disappointment. And, when he does, such reproach is painful, but often it is just what we need to turn us to the right path.

> Do not gloat when your enemy falls; when they stumble, do not let your heart rejoice, or the LORD will see and disapprove and turn his wrath away from them. —Proverbs 24:17–18

> "Therefore, behold, I will surely lift you up and cast you away from my presence, you and the city that I gave to you and your fathers. And I will bring upon you everlasting reproach and perpetual shame, which shall not be forgotten."
> —Jeremiah 23:39–40, ESV

My prayer: Lord, from babyhood, I have been so tenderhearted as to cry when I realized that someone I love and respect has been disappointed in me. I am saddened when I think back at the many ways I have disappointed you, the only one who matters eternally. Thank you for helping me, time and again, to course-correct, and thank you for not turning away from me forever.

When God expresses his disapproval of your actions, how do you respond?

Terrifies

This same loving God who comforts us and assures us is able—and willing—to fill people with terror. He is sovereign. He is almighty. People should revere him and be aware of his ability to command forces that can turn lives upside down.

> God has made my heart faint; the Almighty has terrified me.
> —Job 23:16

> "Get yourself ready! Stand up and say to them whatever I command you. Do not be terrified by them, or I will terrify you before them." —Jeremiah 1:17

My prayer: Lord, I know that your power is dreadful and that I could be terrified before you, but I am convinced that you have saved me for yourself, to be your beloved child, so I have nothing to fear. I am so thankful that I won't feel the need to turn and run futilely when the time of judgment comes. Instead, I know that I can rest in the shadow of your loving wings.

When has something positive happened as a result of something that had terrified you at the time?

Invincible

Just how powerful is God? He is invincible, too powerful to be defeated, now or ever. We can enjoy deep-down assurance knowing that the one true God, our leader, is the only one who cannot be overcome by any physical or spiritual force. He is forevermore the overcomer.

> Who is the King of glory? The LORD, strong and mighty; the LORD, invincible in battle. —Psalm 24:8, NLT

> I know that you can do all things; no purpose of yours can be thwarted. —Job 42:2

> We heard about God's mighty deeds, now we have seen them, in the city of the LORD, the invincible Warrior, in the city of our God. God makes it permanently secure. —Psalm 48:8, NET

My prayer: Almighty God, I know that you are invincible. Nothing is too strong, too difficult, for you to overcome. Thank you for the security of knowing that I am protected by your love and your overwhelming power.

In what way does it relieve you to know that God is invincible?

Turns us around

God knows what is best for us, and often that requires us to do an about-face. He asks us to change our attitude or behavior, so that we can be transformed to be more and more like Jesus. After God turns us around, we are better able to fulfill the good purpose he has custom-made us to do.

> He uncovers their ears at that time and terrifies them with warnings, in order to turn a person from his actions and suppress his pride. —Job 33:16–17, HCSB

> If my people, who are called by my name, will humble themselves and pray and seek my face and turn from their wicked ways, then I will hear from heaven, and I will forgive their sin and will heal their land. —2 Chronicles 7:14

My prayer: Good Shepherd, you loved me enough to turn me around. You prodded me to have a good look at myself. You allowed me to get to the point at which I begged for you to show me the way. Yes, I was ready. You turned me around, and you showed me how to take the first step, then the next step, and the next, on my new path. I will praise you forever.

When has God asked you to turn around in behavior or attitude and get on a better track?

Models

In Jesus, God has shown us a perfect example to follow. As we follow that example, God is fashioning us, refining us, and transforming us into someone who is increasingly beautiful.

> Very truly I tell you, whoever believes in me will do the works
> I have been doing [modeling], and they will do even greater
> things than these, because I am going to the Father. —John 14:12

> Follow God's example, therefore, as dearly loved children and walk
> in the way of love, just as Christ loved us and gave himself up for
> us as a fragrant offering and sacrifice to God. —Ephesians 5:1–2

My prayer: Lord, thank you for sending your Son to be a physical, human model for us. In your wisdom, you sent him to teach us, to demonstrate to us how to live. His perfect life culminated in perfect obedience as he agreed to be sacrificed for us. Thank you for equipping me more and more each day to reflect your glory to those around me. Like a lump of clay, I am being modeled from something quite unattractive, into a better version of myself, the version you have in mind.

What person in your life has shown you an admirable example that helped transform you?

Brightens

God lights up our paths, making the dark places safer. Even a small amount of his light makes things feel more secure and less gloomy for us. God brightens our outlook, too, illuminating our minds and our lives with his truth.

> But now for a brief moment favor has been shown by the LORD our God, to leave us a remnant and to give us a secure hold within his holy place, that our God may brighten our eyes and grant us a little reviving in our slavery. —Ezra 9:8, ESV

> For it is you who light my lamp; the LORD my God lightens my darkness. —Psalm 18:28, ESV

My prayer: Lord, you not only add light, you created light, and that makes it good. In your perfect wisdom, you brighten the dark places in my life. I pray that you will brighten my path and enlighten me today, so that I do not stumble about. Instead, may my actions declare that I belong to you.

In what ways has God brightened the path ahead of you?

Reveals/unveils

Nothing is secret from God; he knows all. In his own wisdom and timing, God chooses to make known to us things that had been previously unknown. He unveils insights and enables understanding. He reveals himself and his truth in amounts—and timing—that we can bear.

> He reveals the deep and hidden things; he knows what lies in the darkness, and light dwells with him. —Daniel 2:22

> He reveals the deep things of darkness and brings utter darkness into the light. —Job 12:22

> He who forms the mountains, who creates the wind, and who reveals his thoughts to mankind, who turns dawn to darkness, and treads on the heights of the earth—the LORD God Almighty is his name. —Amos 4:13

My prayer: Father, thank you for revealing yourself to me through Scripture, through song, and through the people you have put in my life who teach me your truth. Your very creation declares your glory and your might. Your word increasingly enlightens me, uplifts me, and guides me. I am so grateful that I am on this side of the resurrection, that you have revealed the good news. Without this, I would simply be plodding along from day to day without you, without hope.

How have God's revelations had an impact on your life?

Reconciles

Meaning "restores to harmonious relationship," the word *reconciles* ushers in the gospel message: every one of us is sinful; being sinful, we cannot enter God's holy presence, but Jesus' death made reconciliation possible. Christ's sacrifice on the cross was the only satisfactory payment for our sins. If we believe that is true, God welcomes us into his presence.

> Once you were alienated from God and were enemies in your minds because of your evil behavior. But now he has reconciled you by Christ's physical body through death to present you holy in his sight, without blemish and free from accusation.
> —Colossians 1:21–22

> For if, while we were God's enemies, we were reconciled to him through the death of his Son, how much more, having been reconciled, shall we be saved through his life! —Romans 5:10

My prayer: Merciful and loving Lord, my soul was not at peace until you reconciled me to yourself. Thank you for the great gift, the sacrifice of your Son, that showed me the depth of your love, the extent to which you would go to eliminate the chasm between me and you. I was far away from you, and you brought me into a harmonious relationship with you. Thank you for the immeasurable gift of reconciliation.

How have seemingly unreconcilable differences affected you?

Works all things together for good

God's complexities and his goodness are unlimited. The way he works to-gether everything in this universe—every person's plan, interwoven at just the right time with just the right circumstances—is a miracle. And he does it continuously and for our good.

> You intended to harm me, but God intended it for good to
> accomplish what is now being done, the saving of many lives.
> —Genesis 50:20

> And we know that in all things God works for the good of
> those who love him, who have been called according to his
> purpose. —Romans 8:28

My prayer: Lord, you are sovereign over all things. And you are good. Therefore, I know that you might make or let things happen that do not seem to be toward the end that I have in mind. But you control everything. You prevent ultimate evil. Your plan is to save and protect me because you love me and I love you. Help me trust in your almighty hand when things don't seem to go "my way" and to trust you in all things.

What was a time when you saw that God had made many pieces come to-gether toward a good end?

Adored/worshiped

For who he is, for all he has done, God is so worthy of our reverence, worship, and intense admiration. How blessed we are to enjoy a personal relationship with him and to have the opportunity to worship him privately or openly in a group. Moreover, our acts of service and outward attitudes confirm our reverence for him.

> Come, let us bow down in worship, let us kneel before the
> LORD our Maker. —Psalm 95:6

> And all the angels stood round about the throne, and the ancients, and the four living creatures; and they fell down before the throne upon their faces, and adored God.
> —Revelation 7:11, DRB

My prayer: My Lord and my God, I know that you are with me now, and I can only imagine what it will be like in heaven when I am in your glorious presence. At that time, I really do not think I will be looking to be reunited with others from my earthly life. I can only think that I will be adoring you, worshiping you with all of my heart, soul, mind, and strength, forever proclaiming your greatness.

Describe a time when you experienced a particularly meaningful time of worship.

Unsearchable/unfathomable

We may yearn to thoroughly know God, but the fact is, we are incapable of fully exploring or completely understanding God. Our incapability stems from the fact that we start from our human point of view, which is limited, while he is infinite. Although it is impossible to get to the bottom of such a quest, it is also wonderful to keep on seeking because it reassures us of our God's vastness.

> Call to me and I will answer you and tell you great and un-searchable things you do not know. —Jeremiah 33:3

> He has made everything beautiful in its time. He has also set eternity in the human heart; yet no one can fathom what God has done from beginning to end. —Ecclesiastes 3:11

My prayer: Great God, the more I know, the more I realize how little I know. I want to know more and more about you, your character, your wonderful deeds. There is no end to your greatness and love, no end to the miracles you have performed on behalf of those who love you and indeed, on my behalf. Thank you, my great, great, unfathomable God.

Express some ways in which you would like to go deeper in relationship with God.

All in all

We cannot fathom God's omnipresence, his all-pervasive nature, nor his all-encompassing love and power. Yet if we have even an inkling of who he is, we can be assured that he is everything we need for every aspect of our lives. He is our source, our refuge, and our complete hope for all eternity. He is sovereign over all things, and he will receive the ultimate glory.

> When he has done this [put everything under Christ's feet],
> then the Son himself will be made subject to him who put
> everything under him, so that God may be all in all.
> —1 Corinthians 15:28

> So that neither the planter nor the waterer is of any impor-
> tance. God who gives the increase is all in all.
> —1 Corinthians 3:7, WEY

My prayer: Lord, you are all. You are everywhere at all times, and you know all things forever, all things present, past, and future. You are all-powerful; you created all things. You have a plan for all, and I know you have a plan for me. Your love pervades all you have made, and your scope is beyond anything I can imagine. I cannot grasp even a modicum of all you are, yet I know full well that you are great beyond measure. You deserve all of the praise and glory for all time.

What can you do to make God more fully your all?

Complete/absolute

God lacks nothing. Nothing can be added to him or his abilities, for he is complete. Infinite in power, mercy, and love, with a perfect view of truth in all things, he has total authority, with absolute justice, over all.

> LORD, Your testimonies are completely reliable; holiness is the beauty of Your house for all the days to come.
> —Psalm 93:5, HCSB

> And God placed all things under his feet and appointed him to be head over everything for the church, which is his body, the fullness [completeness] of him who fills everything in every way. —Ephesians 1:22–23

> But of His Son, He says, "Thy throne, O God, is for ever and for ever, and the sceptre of Thy Kingdom is a sceptre of absolute justice." —Hebrews 1:8, WEY

My prayer: Almighty God, in today's world of "there are no absolutes," I am confident that there is one: your word is absolute. Your word is truth. Your word lays out what is best. You, Lord, are everything I need. Completely. Absolutely. You have made a plan for me that is right and complete and true in every way. And you have made me to fit that plan. Thank you for the certainty of your absolutes and the truth of your love.

How does knowing God is complete and absolute affect your outlook?

Silent

Though God is sometimes silent, he is never far away. He is always attentive to our cry. Sometimes he isn't quick to provide an answer. Silence might mean "not yet," which is a valid answer to a question. His silence may be telling us to dig deeper to better understand his truth or his purposes. Or, he may be encouraging us to be still and wait for his wisdom.

> After all this, LORD, will you hold yourself back? Will you keep silent and punish us beyond measure? —Isaiah 64:12

> O God, do not remain silent; do not turn a deaf ear, do not stand aloof, O God. —Psalm 83:1b

> But if he remains silent, who can condemn him? If he hides his face, who can see him? Yet he is over individual and nation alike. —Job 34:29

My prayer: Lord, there are times when you remain silent, but I know that you are still with me; you love me, and you hear me. I need not be afraid in times of your holy silence. Help me to be patient during these times. Thank you for your wisdom as you use your silence for your good purposes.

How do you deal with silence when what you really want is an answer?

Faithful

God is true to his word. He promises to love, comfort, protect, and deliver us. He promises to never leave nor forsake us. We can be confident of these things because he has proven throughout the ages to be ever-faithful.

> Know therefore that the LORD your God is God; he is the faithful God, keeping his covenant of love to a thousand generations of those who love him and keep his commandments. —Deuteronomy 7:9

> But the Lord is faithful, and he will strengthen you and protect you from the evil one. —2 Thessalonians 3:3

> Let us hold unswervingly to the hope we profess, for he who promised is faithful. —Hebrews 10:23

My prayer: Steadfast God, the examples in the Bible of your faithfulness became relevant to me and more relatable when I began to trust in you. I trust what you say because you are unfailingly good and have my best interest in mind. You have a plan for good in my life, and I praise you for your faithfulness.

How is God's faithfulness relevant and relatable to you?

Abundant/bounteous

Because of God's extreme lovingkindness toward us, he blesses us abundantly. He freely bestows his goodness, grace, mercy, and every good thing. When we live in such bounty, it should follow that we let our blessings overflow to others.

> And God is able to bless you abundantly, so that in all things at all times, having all that you need, you will abound in every good work. —2 Corinthians 9:8

> You crown the year with a bountiful harvest; even the hard pathways overflow with abundance. —Psalm 65:11, NLT

> They feast on the abundance of your house; you give them drink from your river of delights. —Psalm 36:8

My prayer: My Lord, you provide bounteously everything that I need and far above anything that I could have imagined. You have given everything so freely, even to the extent of giving your Son as an atoning sacrifice for my sin. Your goodness and love are infinite, and as I continue to delve into your word, I am more and more aware of the abundance of your provision and am pleased, in turn, to share. Thank you!

What aspect of God's abundance particularly blesses you?

Sufficiency

God is all we need. He perfectly satisfies all of the essentials for our daily living, both physically and spiritually. With him, we have enough and are not left wanting.

> Not that we are sufficient in ourselves to claim anything as coming from us, but our sufficiency is from God.
> —2 Corinthians 3:5, ESV

> But he said to me, "My grace is sufficient for you, for my power is made perfect in weakness." —2 Corinthians 12:9a

> His divine power has given us everything we need for a godly life through our knowledge of him who called us by his own glory and goodness. —2 Peter 1:3

My prayer: Lord, please forgive me when I act according to the notion that *you+something* will prevail. Everything about you is sufficient to overflowing. All I need is in you. I praise you for showing me the truth that you are more than enough.

When you were fully trusting in God, in what way have you ever found him to be insufficient or just not enough to satisfy your needs?

Unhurried

Though he is able to, and often does, act in a split second, we can be assured that God's movements have "just-right" timing. Because we cannot see the big picture, we may consider his timing to be fast or slow, but the truth is that his timing is perfect. Everything he does coordinates with other actions to meet his divine purpose.

> But do not forget this one thing, dear friends: With the Lord
> a day is like a thousand years, and a thousand years are like a
> day. The Lord is not slow in keeping his promise, as some un-
> derstand slowness. Instead he is patient with you, not wanting
> anyone to perish, but everyone to come to repentance.
> —2 Peter 3:8–9

> This vision is for a future time. It describes the end, and it will
> be fulfilled. If it seems slow in coming, wait patiently, for it will
> surely take place. It will not be delayed. —Habakkuk 2:3, NLT

My prayer: Lord, you demonstrate patience to me so that I can learn and be more like you. Sadly, I am often rushing around. Many times I have proceeded on *my* timing, only to find out later that your timing would have been so much better. Thank you for your counsel to wait upon you. I am so blessed to know that although your timing is not the same as *my* timing, your timing is always perfect.

When has God taking his own sweet time actually turned out to be a blessing to you?

Leads

Because God is sovereign, he has command over all things. Omniscient, he knows the best way to go and moves us forward in the right direction. He holds our hand and shines a light on our path, so that we are able to take one step after another and not get ahead of ourselves.

> And the LORD was going before them in a pillar of cloud by day to lead them on the way, and in a pillar of fire by night to give them light, that they might travel by day and by night.
> —Exodus 13:21, NASB 2020

> But he brought his people out like a flock; he led them like sheep through the wilderness. —Psalm 78:52

> For You are my rock and my fortress; For the sake of Your name You will lead me and guide me.
> —Psalm 31:3, NASB 2020

My prayer: Lord, you are the perfect leader. Only you know the way, the best way, the right way. I am so glad that you are my leader. I can trust you to show me the way that is best for me, the way that is in your perfect will and according to your plan.

What one area of your life are you even a little bit reluctant to turn over to God's leadership?

Pathmaker

God not only leads us along the path that is best for us, he makes the path. His path is the best way to go from Point A to Point B, preventing a lot of wasted time and motion. We don't have to stumble over rocky trails; his smooth, straight paths make our way easier.

> In their hearts humans plan their course, but the LORD establishes their steps. —Proverbs 16:9
>
> I instruct you in the way of wisdom and lead you along straight paths. —Proverbs 4:11
>
> Trust in the LORD with all your heart and lean not on your own understanding; in all your ways submit to him, and he will make your paths straight. —Proverbs 3:5–6

My prayer: I trust you, Lord, for you have proven to be righteous and loving. It is not too late for me; you have put me on the right path. I pray that I will be sensitive to your leading, so that I may continue to walk the path you have planned just for me.

When have you gone "the long way around" rather than going the better way that God had in mind for you?

Compels/constrains

Because God loves us and because he has the divine view of the future, he nudges—he urges—us toward the calling that he has prepared for us. He wants us to live for him, and he has equipped us to choose a particular course of action.

> For I am full of words, and the spirit within me compels me.
> —Job 32:18

> But when Silas and Timothy came down from Macedonia, Paul was constrained by the word, testifying to the Jews that Jesus was the Christ. —Acts 18:5, ERV

> For Christ's love compels us, because we are convinced that one died for all, and therefore all died. And he died for all, that those who live should no longer live for themselves but for him who died for them and was raised again. —2 Corinthians 5:14–15

My prayer: I praise you, Lord, that the things that compelled me in the past are not in force today. Your Spirit urges me to share your love and your perfect plan for salvation. I recognize those silent nudges as coming from you. Thank you for your hand on my life.

When do you think the Holy Spirit has compelled you to do or say something?

Close/near

God is always nearby, right with us. We can feel his nearness. It is true that he fills the heavens, yet he is not a faraway god that we must call to loudly in order to gain his attention. He is so near to our hearts that he knows our every need even before we speak.

> But as for me, it is good to be near God. I have made the Sovereign LORD my refuge; I will tell of all your deeds.
> —Psalm 73:28

> The LORD is near to the brokenhearted and saves those who are crushed in spirit. —Psalm 34:18, NASB 2020

> The LORD is near to all who call on him, to all who call on him in truth. —Psalm 145:18

My prayer: Abba, being close to you and having the assurance that you are close to me is heartening. I know that you care for me, and I am grateful that I can rest close to your heart, under the shadow of your loving wing.

When is it most important to you to feel close to someone?

Walks

God walks with us. Our heavenly Father holds us by the hand. He moves along right with us at an unhurried pace, giving us insights about himself and his creation as we walk together.

> Then the man and his wife heard the sound of the LORD God as he was walking in the garden in the cool of the day, and they hid from the LORD God among the trees of the garden.
> —Genesis 3:8

> I will also walk among you and be your God, and you shall be my people. —Leviticus 26:12

My prayer: Father, during so much of my life, I have been in a hurry. But now, I love it that I am walking with you, whether I am literally walking or just going places in my mind. You are with me, right by my side, Immanuel. We are not in a hurry; we are enjoying our fellowship. Thank you for this blessing.

During your life, what did you miss—or what are you missing now—by being in a hurry?

Communes

Communing is sharing thoughts or feelings with intimacy or intensity. In a commune, it is actually living with one another. When we make our hearts ready for God, he comes to live within us, then we get to enjoy a deep sense of intimacy with him as he continues to teach our hearts and minds.

> Jesus replied, "Anyone who loves me will obey my teaching. My Father will love them, and we will come to them and make our home with them." —John 14:23

> And there I will meet with you, and I will commune with you from above the mercy seat, from between the two cherubim which are on the ark of the testimony, of all things which I will give you in commandment to the children of Israel.
> —Exodus 25:22, AKJV

My prayer: Lord, you are the Creator and Sustainer of the universe, yet you want to make your home with me, conversing and sharing your thoughts right into my heart. Thank you. My heart and mind are open to you, and I am so thankful that you want to—and do—commune with me.

How can you bless someone in your life by sharing your intimate thoughts or feelings?

Carries us

Sometimes we just can't do it on our own, whatever "it" is. When we don't have the strength to make it on our own, God bears us up; he transports us (spiritually, emotionally, or physically) from where we are to where we need to be.

> . . . and in the wilderness. There you saw how the LORD your God carried you, as a father carries his son, all the way you went until you reached this place. —Deuteronomy 1:31

> He tends his flock like a shepherd: He gathers the lambs in his arms and carries them close to his heart; he gently leads those that have young. —Isaiah 40:11

My prayer: Merciful Lord, how you have carried me! You majestically swooped down to protect me from evil and from my own bad choices. Looking back, I can see some of the times you have carried me when I could not or should not have taken another step. Indeed, your great mercy protects me from actually knowing all of the times you have carried me; if I knew how many, it probably would be too much for me to bear.

Describe a time when you needed God to carry you.

Comforts/consoles

Our compassionate, loving God knows when we are suffering, anxious, or grieving, and he eases the pain we are feeling. He comforts us with reassurances that he is with us, and he consoles us in times of disappointment.

> Even though I walk through the darkest valley, I will fear no evil, for you are with me; your rod and your staff, they comfort me. —Psalm 23:4

> Praise be to the God and Father of our Lord Jesus Christ, the Father of compassion and the God of all comfort, who comforts us in all our troubles, so that we can comfort those in any trouble with the comfort we ourselves receive from God.
> —2 Corinthians 1:3–4

My prayer: Lord, you offer comfort to me any time I ask. Your Holy Spirit is with me, comforting me, reminding me of all you have done and all you are able to do. Thank you for your great love and for knowing just what I need as I draw near for your comfort.

When have you been comforted in a deep and meaningful way?

Finds

God never loses us. We allow ourselves to get lost in the world. Sometimes we are lured by a promise of satisfaction in a place other than with God. And so, he seeks us, and he finds us in that place. When we recognize that we have been lost, it is a thrill to see that God joyfully wants us to reunite with him.

> And when he comes home, he calls together his friends and his neighbors, saying to them, "Rejoice with me, for I have found my sheep that was lost." Just so, I tell you, there will be more joy in heaven over one sinner who repents than over ninety-nine righteous persons who need no repentance.
> —Luke 15:6–7, ESV

> And he said to him [the brother of the prodigal], "Son, you are always with me, and all that is mine is yours. It was fitting to celebrate and be glad, for this your brother was dead, and is alive; he was lost, and is found." —Luke 15:31–32, ESV

My prayer: Lord, I know that you are always aware of where I am, spiritually, emotionally, and physically. Yet at times I have been lost. In drawing me to yourself, you "found" me. I praise you for turning my heart in your direction so that I would seek you and find you.

Have you ever been lost? And how were you found?

Repeats

God tells us about his love, and he demonstrates his love to us, over and over again. He repeats the truth of it so that we will not miss the blessing of being in relationship with him.

> For God speaks again and again, though people do not recognize it. —Job 33:14, NLT

> "While you were doing all these things," declares the LORD, "I spoke to you again and again, but you did not listen; I called you, but you did not answer." —Jeremiah 7:13

> Whatever is, has already been, and whatever will be, already is. God repeats what has passed. —Ecclesiastes 3:15, HCSB

My prayer: Lord, it is no wonder you call me one of your sheep. My ability to really learn can be so limited. You tell me things again and again, yet I don't retain what you have said. You show me again and again, and I don't completely change my ways. Thank you for loving me still, even though I apparently need to be told and shown—over and over again—your love, mercy, faithfulness, and all of the rest of your goodness, blessings, and promises.

What truth in your life bears repeating?

Illuminates/lights

God's light shines on our path, to help us through the darkness. He also adds light and understanding to where we stand intellectually, spiritually, and emotionally. He illuminates the deepest part of us, providing light and assurance for each step that we take.

> The sun will no more be your light by day, nor will the brightness of the moon shine on you, for the LORD will be your everlasting light, and your God will be your glory.
> —Isaiah 60:19

> For You are my lamp, LORD; And the LORD illumines my darkness. —2 Samuel 22:29, NASB 2020

My prayer: My God and my King, I cannot see the true path without your light. Thank you for illuminating my heart, as well as helping me to understand some part of the vastness of your love for me. I pray, Lord, that you will continue to show me the way.

Describe a time when the (figurative) light bulb went on intellectually, spiritually, or emotionally. What did you do as a result?

Scoffs

With disdain, God calls out those who think they have any power against him or his purposes. He expresses scorn, laughing at times because our notions are actually stupid or silly, like fashioning our own idol and then worshiping it as though it could do anything for us.

> The One enthroned in heaven laughs; the Lord scoffs at them [those who band against Him]. —Psalm 2:4
>
> . . . but the Lord laughs at the wicked, for he knows their day is coming. —Psalm 37:13
>
> Though he scoffs at the scoffers, yet he gives grace to the needy. —Proverbs 3:34, NASB 2020

My prayer: Lord, I know that the troublemakers of the world are as nothing to you; you scoff at them; you reign supreme. Although you may have scoffed at many of my stupid thoughts and silly actions, thank you for not giving up on me. Instead, you loved me and did not turn me away when I finally reached out to you.

What have you ever done that caused God to scoff? Why does he have the right to scoff?

Convicts

When God finds us to be guilty of something, he lovingly and with perfect justice convinces us of our error or sinfulness. He is able to cut right to the heart of an issue for our good, to help us turn away from our wrong thinking and actions and focus on right living.

> When the people heard this [that God had made Jesus both
> Lord and Messiah and that they had crucified him], they
> were cut to the heart and said to Peter and the other apostles,
> "Brothers, what shall we do?" —Acts 2:37

> See, the Lord is coming with thousands upon thousands of his
> holy ones to judge everyone, and to convict all of them of all
> the ungodly acts they have committed in their ungodliness,
> and of all the defiant words ungodly sinners have spoken
> against him. —Jude 1:14b–15

My prayer: Father, you know when to convict me, pressing down on my spirit to help me see my own wrong. You do this by your Spirit, through your word, and through faithful people who love you and are willing to speak up. Thank you for convicting me of my sinful ways, for your forgiveness, and for your transforming work in my life.

When have you done something wrong and felt convicted to make things right again?

Frustrates

God has his plan, his right and perfect plan. And sometimes he must step in and prevent an attempted action from taking place, so that his plan will be fulfilled without interruption. When we feel frustrated because our own plans just are not working out, it might be that God has something better in mind.

> The LORD brings the counsel of the nations to nothing; he frustrates the plans of the peoples. —Psalm 33:10, ESV

> The LORD watches over the foreigner and sustains the fatherless and the widow, but he frustrates the ways of the wicked. —Psalm 146:9

> He frustrates the plans of schemers so the work of their hands will not succeed. —Job 5:12, NLT

My prayer: My Lord and Savior, how many of my unwise plans have you thwarted as a way of preventing harm to your beloved child? I am certain there have been many. Thank you, my Protector, for frustrating the plans that, then and in the future, would have led me far off course.

When has God thwarted an unwise plan of yours?

Overwhelms/overtakes

It is a wonderful feeling, scary even, when God overwhelms us with his love. The vastness of his love is impossible to fully take in. It washes over us in such a powerful way. Because of his great love, he protects us by overtaking or completely defeating our enemies.

> Therefore, the Lord will overwhelm them with a mighty flood
> from the Euphrates River—the king of Assyria and all his glory.
> This flood will overflow all its channels. —Isaiah 8:7, NLT

> And all these blessings shall come upon you and overtake you,
> if you obey the voice of the LORD your God.
> —Deuteronomy 28:2, ESV

My prayer: Almighty God, the Bible speaks of times when you overwhelmed nations with your power. Those times demonstrated your protection of those you love and your commitment to your great plan of salvation. Lord, my heart and mind are overwhelmed at the greatness of your love, your grace, your mercy, your creativity, your power, your vision, and your plan. I have full confidence that you will use your power for ultimate "good," even for consequences that I dare not even contemplate.

How have you been overwhelmed by good, tender, or adverse circumstances? And then what happened?

Conqueror

Throughout history, God has conquered opposing nations, saving his people from complete destruction. By his power, he has subdued our greatest enemy. Because God knows all, he can promise the ultimate defeat of sin and darkness because victory has already been determined.

> For he says: "By my strong hand I have accomplished this, by my strategy that I devised. I invaded the territory of nations, and looted their storehouses. Like a mighty conqueror, I brought down rulers." —Isaiah 10:13, NET

> The Lord God is my strength: and he will make my feet like the feet of harts: and he the conqueror will lead me upon my high places singing psalms. —Habakkuk 3:19, DRB

My prayer: O Mighty One, you have been a conqueror throughout history. Evil seems overwhelming at times, but you will be the victor in the end. Thank you for sharing in your word examples of your power and might, and for providing a glimpse of your ultimate victory.

In what area of your life do you need God's help in conquering a challenge?

Sets straight

Sometimes things just are not right, and it takes a mighty and loving God to redirect, so that situations and relationships are on target with his purpose. Almighty God is able to set things straight, to set our path straight, to set us straight.

> I will lead the blind by ways they have not known, along un-familiar paths I will guide them; I will turn the darkness into light before them and make the rough places smooth. These are the things I will do; I will not forsake them. —Isaiah 42:16

> For I am ready to set things right, not in the distant future, but right now! I am ready to save Jerusalem and show my glory to Israel. —Isaiah 46:13, NLT

My prayer: Only you, my Lord, can make the rough places smooth, the crooked straight, whether path or people. You have provided the perfect way for my salvation. Thank you for making my path straighter and more level and for showing me the way, the only way, to salvation.

What situation has God set straight for you?

Renews

God makes us new spiritually. Through his living word, he restores our vigor. He reminds us of our many blessings, and that renews our outlook. He helps us be still when we need to be still. He refreshes us when we spend time in prayer and reflection.

> He will renew your life and sustain you in your old age.
> —Ruth 4:15a

> Create in me a pure heart, O God, and renew a steadfast spirit within me. —Psalm 51:10

My prayer: Lord, you gave me choice, and initially, I chose not to follow your ways. I chose to try, under my own strength, to be a good person. Despite my well-meaning philosophy, you allowed me to descend to a very bad place. And, because you know my inmost thoughts and love me, you discerned the readiness of my heart. You answered my call when I asked you to show me the way. You renewed me. You washed me with your righteousness, and I can never be thankful enough for the way that you restored my spirit.

What would you like God to make new, revive, or refresh in your life?

Strengthens

God makes us stronger and helps us grow physically, spiritually, emotionally, and relationally. He gives us the power we need in all situations, including times when we think there is no hope.

> He gives strength to the weary and increases the power of the weak. Even youths grow tired and weary, and young men stumble and fall; but those who hope in the LORD will renew their strength. —Isaiah 40:29–31a

> It is God who arms me with strength and keeps my way secure. —Psalm 18:32

> I can do all this through him who gives me strength. —Philippians 4:13

My prayer: O, my God of love, power, and might, you have so often strengthened me when I had no more strength within me. Thank you for delivering me time and again by providing exactly what I needed.

In what ways do you need to be strengthened today so that you can better serve God?

Avenges

We so often focus on God being loving, good, and patient that we don't consider his ability—and willingness—to avenge. Still, his very goodness requires justice. God will at times inflict harm in return for a wrong done to him or to his people. He does not want us to sin in response to being wronged; with justice and perfect timing, he will address the iniquities.

> It is mine to avenge; I will repay. In due time their foot will slip; their day of disaster is near and their doom rushes upon them.
> —Deuteronomy 32:35

> Then my anger will cease and my wrath against them will subside, and I will be avenged. And when I have spent my wrath on them, they will know that I the LORD have spoken in my zeal. —Ezekiel 5:13

My prayer: I'm so thankful, Lord, that you will judge in your own right timing; you will take care of matters that cause division or injury. I need not worry about avenging my own case or that of a friend. Every day I see more clearly that you desire unity among your people, and I have confidence that you will justly handle any negative situation to direct us toward that unity.

How have you tried to avenge an injustice when it would have been better to allow God to do the avenging?

Surpasses

No matter how high the expectations or standard of excellence, anything—everything—accomplished by God proves to be superior. We can never underestimate the extent of what God is able or willing to do.

> But we have this treasure in jars of clay to show that this all-surpassing power is from God and not from us.
> —2 Corinthians 4:7

> I pray that the eyes of your heart may be enlightened, so that you will know . . . what is the boundless greatness of his power toward us who believe. These are in accordance with the working of the strength of his might.
> —Ephesians 1:18a, 19, NASB 2020

> And the peace of God, which surpasses all understanding, will guard your hearts and your minds in Christ Jesus.
> —Philippians 4:7, ESV

My prayer: Lord, your power, greatness, love, knowledge, wisdom, peace, mercy—all of your attributes—surpass anything that anyone could ever attempt. Thank you for giving me your surpassing grace and for demonstrating to me that you loved me enough to save me.

Think of a time when you underestimated what God would be willing or able to do. What happened?

Never-forsaking

God promises that he will never abandon those who love him. He faithfully stays with us through hard times. His grace abounds in second chances, so he never gives up on us nor turns his back on us.

> Be strong and courageous. Do not be afraid or terrified because of them, for the LORD your God goes with you; he will never leave you nor forsake you. —Deuteronomy 31:6

> No one will be able to stand against you all the days of your life. As I was with Moses, so I will be with you; I will never leave you nor forsake you. —Joshua 1:5

> Keep your life free from love of money, and be content with what you have, for he has said, "I will never leave you nor forsake you." —Hebrews 13:5, ESV

My prayer: Lord, you placed within me the truth of your presence. When I was feeling so alone, there was a small but constant light within me that assured me that I was not alone. Thank you for your promise never to forsake me. With you by my side, I have everything I need. I pray that my loved ones will also know the truth of your constancy and your unfailing Father-love.

How could you explain to a friend or loved one that God will never turn his back on them? How would knowing this basic truth affect that person?

Brilliant/dazzling

God is full of light so bright, so dazzling, that his presence goes beyond intense radiance. If we were to face him right now, our eyes would be blinded. Nevertheless, the hope of one day being with him lies before us, and we yearn to be made ready to be with him.

> I see God moving across the deserts from Edom, the Holy
> One coming from Mount Paran. His brilliant splendor fills the
> heavens, and the earth is filled with his praise.
> —Habakkuk 3:3, NLT

> He lives in light so brilliant that no human can approach him.
> No human eye has ever seen him, nor ever will. All honor and
> power to him forever! Amen. —1 Timothy 6:16b, NLT

My prayer: Lord God Almighty, I cannot imagine approaching you and looking upon your face. Yet I can feel your arms of love, and I find refuge behind your shield of protection. I am certain that you are more spectacular, more brilliant, than I can possibly conceptualize. I will keep on praising you forever.

Contemplate being in the dazzling light of the Lord. What does that feel like?

Indescribable/ineffable

We love God, so naturally we want to tell others about the wonder of him. Made in God's image, we begin to describe him using human terms because that is what we know. While useful as a starting point, this earthly way of trying to make him comprehensible is sorely limited. God is too extreme, too great, and too completely beyond anything in our experience or imagination to be adequately described.

> The LORD is great, and to be praised highly, though his greatness is indescribable. —Psalm 145:3, ISV

> We cannot find him worthily [cannot comprehend him]: he is great in strength, and in judgment, and in justice, and he is ineffable. —Job 37:23, DRB

My prayer: My dear Lord, you have been gracious to continue to reveal to me so many of your attributes, and yet words alone cannot describe you. Actions do speak louder than words, and your involvement in my life has been so deep and moving. I praise you by trying to impart—through my words as well as actions—who you are, so that others will desire to be in right relationship with you.

Through your actions how can you begin to describe God to people who don't know him?

Sovereign

There is a power struggle going on. Human rulers think they are in control, but this is God's universe. He possesses ultimate power and has dominion over every individual and every nation, for his good purposes. His infinite wisdom and goodness direct his power, so we should delight in acknowledging and submitting to his sovereignty.

> O LORD, you are great, mighty, majestic, magnificent, glorious, and sovereign over all the sky and earth! You have dominion and exalt yourself as the ruler of all. —1 Chronicles 29:11, NET

> Then God said to him, "I am the sovereign God. Be fruitful and multiply! A nation—even a company of nations—will descend from you; kings will be among your descendants!"
> —Genesis 35:11, NET

My prayer: Almighty God, it went against my sin nature to let you have complete control of my life. It was, and is, so infantile of me to think that I can control anything. But, Sovereign Lord, thanks to your welcoming grace and forgiveness, I now agree that it is your rightful place to be King of my life. Trusting in you and submitting to your control brings me tremendous freedom and joy.

What part of you still does not want God to be the boss of every single thing in your life?

Rules/reigns

God is ruler over all things. He sits on the heavenly throne, and his kingdom will never end. He does allow us to choose for ourselves whom we will serve. When we submit to his rule and agree that his plan for our lives is best, we can be assured of everlasting peace.

> The LORD has established his throne in heaven, and his kingdom rules over all. —Psalm 103:19

> Then I heard what sounded like a great multitude, like the roar of rushing waters and like loud peals of thunder, shouting: "Hallelujah! For our Lord God Almighty reigns."
> —Revelation 19:6

My prayer: O God, you are great and mighty and wonderful. You created all, and forever you will reign over all of creation. I worship you now, and I look forward to worshiping you when I see you on your heavenly throne. What a marvelous experience that will be. If I am not stunned speechless by your grandeur and impressiveness, I will join the angels in singing "Hallelujah!"

Try to describe how it will feel to approach the throne of the ruler over all things.

Wise

All-wise God is able to perfectly judge each situation as to what is true and right; being omniscient, he knows the end point, not just the current circumstances. When we receive godly wisdom—being pure, merciful, and willing to submit to others—that is different from and better than trusting worldly wisdom which can be competitive, reliant on logic, and self-exalting.

> But the wisdom that comes from heaven is first of all pure;
> then peace-loving, considerate, submissive, full of mercy and
> good fruit, impartial and sincere. —James 3:17

> By wisdom the LORD laid the earth's foundations, by understanding he set the heavens in place. —Proverbs 3:19

> It is because of him that you are in Christ Jesus, who has
> become for us wisdom from God—that is, our righteousness,
> holiness, and redemption. —1 Corinthians 1:30

My prayer: O Lord, my God, I cannot even begin to fathom how great your wisdom is. You created everything from nothing. From before the beginning, you knew that humankind would fall to the power of sin. Because of your plan of salvation—the only way to escape sin's condemnation—I do not have to suffer eternal separation from you. Only someone so wise, so merciful, and so unfathomably loving could have made a way for me to be in relationship with you into eternity.

What wise person have you known and admired, and what made them wise in your eyes?

Patient

God is so loving that he is willing to tolerate delays as people put off turning their hearts toward him and instead keep on sinning. People do not understand the depth of joy they are missing as they continue to avoid having a relationship with him. Yet he patiently waits to bless them.

> Or do you show contempt for the riches of his kindness, forbearance and patience, not realizing that God's kindness is intended to lead you to repentance? —Romans 2:4

> And remember, our Lord's patience gives people time to be saved. This is what our beloved brother Paul also wrote to you with the wisdom God gave him. —2 Peter 3:15, NLT

> What if God, although choosing to show his wrath and make his power known, bore with great patience the objects of his wrath—prepared for destruction? What if he did this to make the riches of his glory known to the objects of his mercy, whom he prepared in advance for glory . . . —Romans 9:22–23

My prayer: Yahweh, I am so thankful that *your* timing is not *my* timing. Under my timing, I surely would have perished before you had the chance to rescue me. Because of your patience, you were willing to wait for me to turn my face toward you and away from my sinful ways. Now I see that your love and patience extend to the point where you *long* to be gracious to the undeserving. Only a God as great as you would have a love so deep.

During the past year, have you grown in patience or lost ground? Why do you think that is?

Lovingkindness

God expresses all of his attributes all the time. He is always kind, always merciful, always gracious, and these flow out from his overarching love. God's lovingkindness is a combination of his heart attitude of kindness and his outward actions based in love.

> How excellent is thy lovingkindness, O God! therefore the children of men put their trust under the shadow of thy wings.
> —Psalm 36:7, KJV

> The LORD is compassionate and gracious, slow to anger and abounding in lovingkindness. He will not always strive with us, nor will he keep his anger forever. He has not dealt with us according to our sins, nor rewarded us according to our iniquities. For as high as the heavens are above the earth, so great is his lovingkindness toward those who fear him.
> —Psalm 103:8–11, NASB 1995

My prayer: Abba, you have surely shown your great and perfect lovingkindness toward me since before I was born. Your mercy is over all that you have made, and I see so many ways you have expressed your great mercy and kindness in my life. I know that what I have seen is not even a fraction of the full extent to which you have lavished your lovingkindness on me. Thank you, my great and loving Father.

How have you shown lovingkindness to a person outside of your family?

Desires

God doesn't need anything, but he strongly wishes to have our hearts. He desires that we long for a true, loving, deep relationship with him. He wants us to be devoted to him and to live righteously, with kindness and mercy to all.

> Like water spilled on the ground, which cannot be recovered, so we must die. But that is not what God desires; rather, he devises ways so that a banished person does not remain banished from him. —2 Samuel 14:14

> For I desire mercy, not sacrifice, and acknowledgment of God rather than burnt offerings. —Hosea 6:6

My prayer: Lord, you have my heart. I love you. I regret that some of my focus is drawn away by day-to-day practicalities. And I confess that my sin nature and the influences of sin in the world get in the way of my being a perfect representative of your goodness, as you deserve. Thank you for the work you are continually doing to strengthen me and refine me. I do deeply yearn to be the person you desire me to be.

In what ways have you made progress during the past year in deepening your relationship with God? How can you build on that?

Values

God esteems us so highly that he sent his Son to save us from the consequences of our sinful choices. When we love Jesus and when our refined inner beauty shows itself in things like integrity, faithfulness, humility, respect, and moral excellence, God is pleased. These are among many things he values in us.

> Since you are precious and honored in my sight, and because I love you, I will give people in exchange for you, nations in exchange for your life. —Isaiah 43:4

> Instead, it [your beauty] should be the inner disposition of the heart, consisting in the imperishable quality of a gentle and quiet spirit, which God values greatly. —1 Peter 3:4, ISV

My prayer: Lord, I know that without Jesus' cloak of righteousness, it is impossible for me to be in your holy presence. Your grace and the sacrifice of your Son have demonstrated that I am immensely valuable to you. Please help me to exhibit the gentle and quiet spirit that is fitting for one who is valued by you.

Which of your attributes do you think God values most? How can you make his investment in you grow?

Calls/beckons

All of us have been called by God, whether or not we choose to hear and respond to that call. He gives us a sign, a dream, a gentle whisper, and he offers his invitation to join him in the work he has prepared for us.

> For the promise is for you and for your children and for all who are far off, everyone whom the Lord our God calls to himself. —Acts 2:39, ESV

> Forgetting what is behind and straining toward what is ahead, I press on toward the goal to win the prize for which God has called me heavenward in Christ Jesus. —Philippians 3:13b–14

My prayer: Thank you, Lord, for beckoning me; you called me to yourself, inviting me to a life of unimaginable richness, love, assurance, and joy. I regret that I did not recognize and respond to your invitation sooner, but I am glad that I have not missed the blessings you have provided since my "yes" to your invitation.

What do you think is your higher calling? How are you responding to that invitation?

Promises/guarantees

Through his word and proven by his faithful—sometimes miraculous—actions, God assures us that he will definitely do what he has promised. The Bible is full of God's promises, and he will keep every one.

> We tell you the good news: What God promised our ancestors he has fulfilled for us, their children, by raising up Jesus. As it is written in the second Psalm: "You are my son; today I have become your father." —Acts 13:32–33

> The Spirit is God's guarantee that he will give us the inheritance he promised and that he has purchased us to be his own people. He did this so we would praise and glorify him. —Ephesians 1:14, NLT

My prayer: Lord, my God, you are faithful in all you do, so with 100 percent confidence I know that you will keep your promises to me. People say, "In this life there are no guarantees," but in you, everything will be as you have said. The more I know about what you have promised, the more I rejoice!

Which of God's promises are most important to you?

Infuses

By his own supernatural power, God breathes good things into our lives. He fills us with hope and joy, instilling in us inner strength and supernatural peace.

> This is what the sovereign LORD says to these bones: Look, I am about to infuse breath into you and you will live.
> —Ezekiel 37:5, NET

> May you be infused with strength and purity, filled with confidence in the presence of God our Father when our Master Jesus arrives with all his followers. —1 Thessalonians 3:13, TM

My prayer: Lord God, my Creator, you have infused me with life, with strength, and with the power of the Holy Spirit. Your word provides the wisdom that I need. Thank you for saving me so that I may be fully responsive to your infusions into my life. I want my life to reflect your goodness.

If you have welcomed the Holy Spirit into your heart, you have been filled with strength. In what way do you see that infusion at work in you?

Shares

Our compassionate God shares in our suffering; carrying part of our burden is one of his gifts to us. God also gives us generous portions from his bounty, sharing with us everything we need, here and now. In eternity, we will be blessed to share in his glory; we will be astonished when we see how he has surrounded us with abundant blessings.

> And because of his glory and excellence, he has given us great and precious promises. These are the promises that enable you to share his divine nature and escape the world's corruption caused by human desires. —2 Peter 1:4, NLT

> Now if we are children, then we are heirs—heirs of God and co-heirs with Christ, if indeed we share in his sufferings in order that we may also share in his glory. —Romans 8:17

My prayer: Lord, thank you for sharing your love, wisdom, and eternity with me. I do not need anything other nor anything more than that. You have filled me to overflowing. Thank you for the assurance that if I must share in your suffering, even a little bit, you will also provide the strength I require to endure it.

God has generously shared so many blessings with us. For which portions from his bounty are you most grateful?

Intimate

God knows us so well that he is the ultimate confidante. When we decide to belong to him, we are blessed to become increasingly close to him in personal and private ways. As we do that, we enjoy a unique, deep, and satisfying relationship.

> Come near to God and he will come near to you. —James 4:8a

> Before they call I will answer; while they are still speaking I will hear. —Isaiah 65:24

My prayer: Lord, it is one of your countless wonders that you would want to have an in-depth friendship with me. You know me so intimately that you perceive what I am thinking before I speak. You are completely aware of everything about me, and you speak into my heart. I cherish the tender intimacy that I have with you who are simultaneously King of the universe and my Abba.

Do you have an intimate, heart-to-heart relationship with someone? How do you nurture that affinity?

Whispers

Sometimes the Bible describes God's voice as "thunder," and yet it also tells of him speaking very softly, whispering to us privately, tenderly. We miss a tremendous blessing when we allow ourselves to become so wrapped up in our own activities that we cannot hear as he whispers into our heart.

> A word was secretly brought to me, my ears caught a whisper of it. —Job 4:12

> And these are but the outer fringe of his works; how faint the whisper we hear of him! Who then can understand the thunder of his power? —Job 26:14

> This is what we speak, not in words taught us by human wisdom but in words taught by the Spirit, explaining spiritual realities with Spirit-taught words. —1 Corinthians 2:13

My prayer: Lord, sometimes your words come to me in a dream, sometimes when I am conscious, and when it happens, I know that it is you speaking your will or insight into my life at that moment. Thank you for your gentle whisper at just the right times.

When have you heard a gentle whisper that told you something that was very important?

Binds up

God perceives all of our injuries of the heart and the body, and he knows perfectly how to heal each one. He holds us tightly while we grieve, and he bandages up our wounds in order for those wounds to heal.

> The moon will shine like the sun, and the sunlight will be seven times brighter, like the light of seven full days, when the LORD binds up the bruises of his people and heals the wounds he inflicted. —Isaiah 30:26

> He heals the brokenhearted and binds up their wounds. —Psalm 147:3

My prayer: Thank you, Great Healer, that you know just how to treat my wounds, my griefs. It gives me comfort and allows healing when I know that you are near, you are willing, and you are able to help me heal.

When have you helped bind up someone's physical, emotional, or spiritual wounds? How did that feel?

Touches

Immanent, God is right here, involved with us, making direct contact with us. At the right times, he touches the body with healing, the mouth with the right words, the mind with wisdom, and the heart with tenderness.

> Then the LORD reached out his hand and touched my mouth and said to me, "I have put my words in your mouth. See, today I appoint you over nations and kingdoms to uproot and tear down, to destroy and overthrow, to build and to plant."
> —Jeremiah 1:9–10

> While he was speaking to me, I was in a deep sleep, with my face to the ground. Then he touched me and raised me to my feet. —Daniel 8:18

My prayer: Lord, you are close. I feel your touch upon my life. I know that you made all things; you fashioned them to your good purpose. Thank you for touching my heart, my mind, my mouth, and my hands, so that I may do your will.

When have you felt God's touch in your body, mind, or heart?

Upholds

God gives us support in our daily living, especially providing backup when we are attacked by the enemy. When we need it most, God strengthens us. He will not let us fall; he lifts us above the fray.

> . . . for the power of the wicked will be broken, but the LORD upholds the righteous . . . though [the one who delights in the LORD] may stumble, he will not fall, for the LORD upholds him with his hand. —Psalm 37:17, 24

> Because of my integrity you uphold me and set me in your presence forever. —Psalm 41:12

> My soul clings to you; your right hand upholds me. —Psalm 63:8, ESV

My prayer: Loving Lord, the fact that you uphold me and strengthen me shows your power as well as your tender love. I am so blessed to know that you are always near, and you know all of my ways so well that you are ready to catch me when I begin to fall.

When did you need to be upheld recently, who did it, and what difference did it make?

Steadies us

When we are anxious, discouraged, or off-track, and when our knees are weak, God firmly fixes us on solid ground. His word provides stability at all times, especially when we feel we are on shaky ground. God helps us maintain or regain our balance, so that we can keep moving forward.

> When the earth totters, and all its inhabitants, it is I who keep steady its pillars. *Selah.* —Psalm 75:3, ESV

> Keep steady my steps according to your promise, and let no iniquity get dominion over me. —Psalm 119:133, ESV

My prayer: My Lord and Savior, I have felt your steadying hand upon my body, my mind, and my life. I praise and thank you for your direction and protection. I trust that you will be faithful in your promise to keep me, to set me apart for you for all eternity.

When did you require the steadying influence of a friend? How did they help you get back on track?

Anchor

As an anchor provides stability, security, and assurance, God holds us firmly to himself. When our tether to him is short, we don't have to worry about drifting out into turbulent waters where we don't really know where we are; we are safely near him.

> God did this [declared on oath to make his purpose clear] so that, by two unchangeable things in which it is impossible for God to lie, we who have fled to take hold of the hope set before us may be greatly encouraged. We have this hope as an anchor for the soul, firm and secure. —Hebrews 6:18–19a

> For they call themselves after the holy city, and anchor themselves upon the God of Israel; The LORD of hosts is his name. —Isaiah 48:2, KJ2000

My prayer: All-powerful and living Lord, I do put my trust in you. You are my Rock, the solid anchor that will not be moved no matter what storms are swirling. I am so thankful that I can trust in you to hold me steady, to keep me from drifting or being washed away.

Do you have an anchor for your soul? What are the purposes of having such an anchor?

Chastises

Sometimes God must reprimand us with more than a scolding. During those times, he refuses to tolerate our lackadaisical or even rebellious attitude any longer. In love, he rebukes us because he wants something better for us than what we are choosing. His admonishment is not pleasant to receive, but it gets our attention.

> Then I will walk contrary unto you also in fury; and I, even I,
> will chastise you seven times for your sins.
> —Leviticus 26:28, KJV

> A psalm for David, for a remembrance of the sabbath. Rebuke
> me not, O Lord, in thy indignation; nor chastise me in thy
> wrath. —Psalm 38:1–2, DRB

My prayer: Lord, I have deserved chastisement, but you held back, knowing that the deserved harsh rebuke would have broken my spirit. Thank you for knowing just how to discipline me. Please help me accept that your forgiveness is complete, that you remember my sins no more.

In what circumstance did you receive chastisement that actually turned around your pattern of behavior?

Casts away/rejects

Our long-suffering God has every right to reject us, dismissing us as inadequate, appropriate for the discard pile. Patiently, he gives us another chance, time and again. Even so, he knows our hearts, and wise people should be forewarned that his patience may not last forever.

> My God will cast them away because they have not listened to him; and they will be wanderers among the nations.
> —Hosea 9:17, NASB 1995

> There they are, in great terror, where there is no terror! For God scatters the bones of him who encamps against you; you put them to shame, for God has rejected them.
> —Psalm 53:5, ESV

> Cast me not away from your presence, and take not your Holy Spirit from me. —Psalm 51:11, ESV

My prayer: Merciful God, you have forgiven and forgiven. All you asked of me was to turn over my heart to you, and you know that I have done that. I am yours, and I need not beg to be in your presence. Thank you for not casting me away, and for giving me another chance—time and again.

When have you felt rejected? What did you do, if anything, to get into the good graces of those who rejected you?

Pierces/penetrates

Penetrating our hearts as he overcomes our stubborn resistance, God helps us grasp his overwhelming love for us. He shines his light into the darkness, so that we can see his truth.

> In your majesty ride forth victoriously in the cause of truth, humility and justice; let your right hand achieve awesome deeds. Let your sharp arrows pierce the hearts of the king's enemies; let the nations fall beneath your feet. —Psalm 45:4–5

> For the word of God is alive and active. Sharper than any double-edged sword, it penetrates even to dividing soul and spirit, joints and marrow; it judges the thoughts and attitudes of the heart. —Hebrews 4:12

My prayer: Lord, your light and your truth penetrate my heart, exposing and assessing all that is there. I pray that your truth will pierce any remaining darkness that is within me and help me see what I must address and change, so that I may more completely walk in your ways.

What insight or truth has penetrated your heart, changing your way forever?

Scatters

For our good, God may cause us to separate from people, things, or places, so that we are not connected anymore to that particular comfort zone. When that happens, though we are scattered away from the familiar, we are never far from him. Our Good Shepherd keeps us safely in his fold.

> God shall arise, his enemies shall be scattered; and those who hate him shall flee before him! —Psalm 68:1, ESV

> He has performed mighty deeds with his arm; he has scattered those who are proud in their inmost thoughts. —Luke 1:51

My prayer: Wise and loving Lord, you shine your light on sin, causing sinners to scuttle away. You freely give your love to all who will come to you. Thank you for calling me to yourself instead of scattering me to the wind, letting me land where evil can have its full effect. I praise you for my sure knowledge of an eternal place with you.

When have you been separated from a comfort zone, then you found that the separation resulted in a benefit for you?

Refreshes/revitalizes

As God transforms us, he takes away our weariness and gives us new strength and energy, granting new life after rebirth. Knowing there is a plan and an eternal place for us reinvigorates our hearts and minds.

> I will refresh the weary and satisfy the faint. —Jeremiah 31:25

> You gave abundant showers, O God; you refreshed your weary inheritance. —Psalm 68:9

> Therefore repent and turn back, so that your sins may be wiped out, that seasons of refreshing may come from the presence of the Lord. —Acts 3:19, HCSB

My prayer: Loving Father, day by day you yourself refresh me, giving me new life. When I confess and turn away from sinful behavior, you revitalize me. When I am weary or tired, and I focus on you, I find strength and direction. Thank you for loving me and for revitalizing me each day.

Describe a time when you felt refreshed or reinvigorated. How was your outlook changed?

Builds up

When we are convicted of our own sin, we tend to cringe and tear ourselves down. But God uses his word and his workers to build us up spiritually. Sometimes he develops us gradually, by small increments, sometimes in significant leaps, but always for the better. As we improve, our efforts to serve him become more fruitful.

> The LORD builds up Jerusalem; he gathers the outcasts of Israel. —Psalm 147:2, ESV

> I will build you up again, and you, Virgin Israel, will be rebuilt. Again you will take up your timbrels and go out to dance with the joyful. —Jeremiah 31:4

> Now I commit you to God and to the word of his grace, which can build you up and give you an inheritance among all those who are sanctified. —Acts 20:32

My prayer: Lord, you know which speed is best for the building-up process. You also know when a bit of tearing down is necessary to strengthen your work. Thank you for continuing to work on me, tearing down as necessary, making adjustments, and building me up to do your work.

What is an example of the process that works best for you: being built up in significant spurts (with rest in between) or being developed gradually?

Shapes/molds

Throughout our lives, God shapes and molds each of us in a particular way. He doesn't use a cookie cutter. When we yield to him, he fashions each of us into the person he wants us to be. The great thing is that God doesn't just make us look good on the outside, he transforms us from the inside out.

> The Spirit of God has made me; the breath of the Almighty gives me life . . . I am the same as you in God's sight; I too am a piece of clay. —Job 33:4, 6

> O house of Israel, can I not do with you as this potter has done? declares the LORD. Behold, like the clay in the potter's hand, so are you in my hand, O house of Israel. —Jeremiah 18:6, ESV

> Yet you, LORD, are our Father. We are the clay, you are the potter; we are all the work of your hand. —Isaiah 64:8

My prayer: Lord, long ago, you formed me within my mother's womb, and you are still shaping me, transforming me. You have in your great mind what you want me to become, and you are refining me daily. Thank you for your vision of me as someone who is pleasing and useful to you.

In what ways have you been uniquely shaped and molded to be pleasing and useful to God?

Amazing

Why are we surprised when God does something astonishing or startlingly impressive? We must only open our eyes to see the amazing things he does in our lives. When it happens, "Wow! Thank you!" and "Praise you!" should be our immediate responses. Because of his marvelous work in our lives, each of us has a compelling testimony to share with others.

> Jesus asked them, "Have you never read in the Scriptures, 'The stone that the builders rejected has become the cornerstone. This was the Lord's doing, and it is amazing in our eyes'?"
> —Matthew 21:42, ISV

> And they sing the song of Moses, the servant of God, and the song of the Lamb, saying, "Great and amazing are your deeds, O Lord God the Almighty! Just and true are your ways, O King of the nations!" —Revelation 15:3, ESV

My prayer: O my great God, everything about you is extraordinary. I could not possibly tell of all of your marvelous deeds in my life, the way that you selected and protected me throughout the years. Thank you for your amazing word that captures just some of what you have done and planned for your people. It is all too wonderful, too powerful for me to convey.

What absolutely amazing work has God done in your life that makes for a compelling testimony to share with others?

Risen

Death has no power over God. Having taken the form of a human, Jesus (the second person of the Godhead) walked this earth with a destiny of dying a humiliating, torturous death. After that death, witnessed by so many and documented for the ages, God raised Jesus to life, as he had promised long before, and Jesus lives in the heavenly realm. He is risen, indeed.

> He is not here; he has risen! Remember how he told you, while he was still with you in Galilee. —Luke 24:6

> We were therefore buried with him through baptism into death in order that, just as Christ was raised from the dead through the glory of the Father, we too may live a new life. —Romans 6:4

My prayer: Yes, Father, I want to be like Jesus, and I embrace your promise that I will rise again—not to tarry on this earth, but that I will rise to be with you. Thank you for raising your Son back to life according to your promise centuries before. And thank you for this powerful witness through Jesus' resurrection that death has no power over you.

Imagine that you are sitting in a quiet place, and you see what you are sure is the risen Christ coming toward you. What is your reaction?

Appears

While in modern life we do not see him physically, as several Old Testament people did, God shows himself to us through his work. His actions are noticeable in our lives. Often using us to reflect a fragment of his character and power, he demonstrates who he is and what he can do.

> When Abram was ninety-nine years old, the LORD appeared to him and said, "I am God Almighty; walk before me faithfully and be blameless." —Genesis 17:1

> That night God appeared to Solomon and said to him, "Ask for whatever you want me to give you." —2 Chronicles 1:7

> The LORD was very angry with Solomon, for his heart had turned away from the LORD, the God of Israel, who had appeared to him twice. —1 Kings 11:9, NLT

My prayer: Ever-present God, it is said that no one can look upon you and live—in this life, anyway. Although I might not see you appear in your full glory here on earth, I know I will see you in eternity. I do see your works here and now. And even though I know you are always present, still I thank you for "showing up" in ways that can only be attributable to you. Your obvious presence deepens my love and strengthens my faith.

In what way(s) has God made his presence known to you recently?

Timeless/perpetual

No matter how hard we try, it is impossible to describe something—some-one—who is beyond our own dimensions of time and space. These are our reference points as humans. But God is beyond any dimensionality, any time frame. Before the beginning, God existed, and he will have no end.

> In time of old You founded the earth, And the heavens are the
> work of Your hands. Even they will perish, but You endure; All
> of them will wear out like a garment; Like clothing You will
> change them and they will pass away. But You are the same,
> and Your years will not come to an end.
> —Psalm 102:25–27, NASB 2020
>
> . . . in the hope of eternal life, which God, who does not lie,
> promised before the beginning of time . . . —Titus 1:2

My prayer: Yahweh, in our finite world people say that "nothing lasts for-ever." But you, Lord, are infinite. You are timeless, perpetual. All of time was and is formed by you and is under your sovereign control. I am honored that before time began, you knew who I would be and how I would fit into your plan. Thank you for this glimpse of the wonder of you.

Although God's timelessness is impossible for a human to truly grasp, in what ways does it matter to you that his existence will have no end?

Crowns

In our world, we strive to be honored. Lest anyone fail to notice, sometimes we even lift ourselves up. Even so, any honor we receive on earth is fleeting. Ultimately, God crowns the humble, giving favor and honor to those who love him, those who acknowledge that they, in themselves, are without resources.

> For the LORD takes delight in his people; he crowns the humble with victory. —Psalm 149:4

> Blessed be the God and Father of our Lord Jesus Christ, who has crowned us with every spiritual blessing in the heavenly realms in Christ. —Ephesians 1:3, WEY

> God blesses those who patiently endure testing and temptation. Afterward they will receive the crown of life that God has promised to those who love him. —James 1:12, NLT

My prayer: Heavenly Father, Jesus wore a painful, humiliating crown of thorns, symbolizing the world's dishonor, and after his crucifixion, you resurrected him, exalting him so that all could see that he is the true King for all eternity. Thank you for the terrible, beautiful truth that Jesus humbled himself on the cross for me, bearing my sin and shame, so that in eternity I can wear the crown of life.

If you have ever been crowned, you know that it can be an uplifting—though fleeting—experience. In what way has God crowned you with lasting favor and honor?

King of kings

God has authority over every single person on this earth. Above any king or ruler, God reigns supreme, having all earthly leaders and all royalty subject under him. Because the Father and the Son "are one" (John 10:30), they are both referred to by the name "King of kings."

> For God is the King of all the earth; sing to him a psalm of praise. —Psalm 47:7
>
> . . . which God will bring about in his own time—God, the blessed and only Ruler, the King of kings and Lord of lords. —1 Timothy 6:15
>
> On his robe and on his thigh he has this name written: King of kings and Lord of lords. —Revelation 19:16

My prayer: Almighty God, the kings of this world see and feel their own power over their realms, but wise kings recognize that *you* have all power and authority over everyone and everything, now and in eternity. Woe to the ruler who does not acknowledge your divine right and sovereignty. For yours is the kingdom, the power, and the glory forever.

In what ways do you honor or praise God as King above all earthly kings?

Adonai/Master

The plural form of the divine name *Adon* meaning "Master" or "Lord," *Adonai* is the covenant name for God among his people. It signifies that he is the master, even owner, of our lives. He guides and protects us, and he deserves our complete obedience.

> I said to the LORD, "You are my Master! Every good thing I have comes from you." —Psalm 16:2, NLT

> And masters, treat your slaves in the same way. Do not threaten them, since you know that he who is both their Master and yours is in heaven, and there is no favoritism with him. —Ephesians 6:9

My prayer: Lord, I am so thankful that you are my master. At one time I was a slave to sin, but you liberated me. Now, I am free and alive in you. I gladly submit to your sovereign control because you desire goodness in my life. I trust you and am pleased to serve you only.

In what ways is it good to have God as your master, the owner, of your life?

Kind

God's nature is that of helpfulness, benevolence, consideration, even indulgence. And yet when God knows that our sought-after answer to a prayer will not be best for us, his "no" is actually a kind response. The depth of his kindness to us is unlike anything we could ever imagine or deserve.

> The LORD is righteous in all his ways and kind in all his works.
> —Psalm 145:17, ESV

> But show me unfailing kindness like the LORD's kindness as long as I live. —1 Samuel 20:14a

> Consider therefore the kindness and sternness of God: sternness to those who fell, but kindness to you, provided that you continue in his kindness. Otherwise, you also will be cut off. —Romans 11:22

My prayer: You set such an unreachable bar, Lord, in kindness. Almost anyone can be nice (polite to others). Kindness is deeper, showing that one truly cares. Because of your kindness and patience, I am able to freely live for you. You demonstrated to me that, no matter what, kindness is better than any other response.

What kindnesses of God's have been especially meaningful to you? In what ways do you exhibit kindness to others?

Gentle

God welcomes us with his gracious and tender nature. Although his power is unlimited, in his unbounded love and wisdom, he demonstrates to us the power of gentleness. He gently loves us into his kingdom.

> Take my yoke upon you and learn from me, for I am gentle and humble in heart, and you will find rest for your souls.
> —Matthew 11:29

> But the fruit of the Spirit is love, joy, peace, patience, kindness, goodness, faithfulness, gentleness and self-control; against such things there is no law. —Galatians 5:22–23

My prayer: Almighty Lord, you are a God of contrasts. You are a God of such extraordinary power. You can move mountains (after all, you created them), yet you have been so gentle and welcoming to me. I am so grateful that in love, you were kind and gentle. In spite of your mighty power, you did not scare me away; in spite of your holiness, you did not pass me by.

Gentleness is a quiet, loving way that seems lost in much of our culture. In what ways do you exhibit gentleness to others?

Benevolent

Out of love and compassion, and as an example for us to follow, God freely shares his great treasures with us. He is not compelled to do so; it flows out of his goodness. He so generously provides everything we need because he truly desires to promote our happiness and wellbeing.

> For God so loved the world that he gave his one and only Son, that whoever believes in him shall not perish but have eternal life. —John 3:16

> . . . that we may live peaceful and quiet lives in all godliness and holiness. This is good, and pleases God our Savior, who wants all people to be saved and to come to a knowledge of the truth. —1 Timothy 2:2b–4

My prayer: Lord, you saw me in my poor state, and through Christ you modeled how to respond generously to those who are in need. Even so, and in view of your abundant gifts, while I am generous, I confess that I do not give sacrificially. Please help me to be more sensitive and responsive to the needs of others. I want to be more like Jesus, reflecting your goodness and benevolence, sharing even more of the resources you have so generously made available to me.

What things has God provided for your happiness and wellbeing? In what ways are you generous in responding to the needs of others?

Forms

When God created the world, he made it from nothing. He created various elements and then brought them together to form everything that exists. He fashioned each thing and every being with infinite attention to detail, knowing how all of it would fit together. Even now, God continues to unite people and circumstances for his good purposes.

> I form the light and create darkness, I bring prosperity and create disaster; I, the LORD, do all these things. —Isaiah 45:7
>
> For this is what the LORD says—he who created the heavens, he is God; he who fashioned and made the earth, he founded it; he did not create it to be empty, but formed it to be inhabited— he says: "I am the LORD, and there is no other." —Isaiah 45:18
>
> I knew you before I formed you in your mother's womb. Before you were born I set you apart and appointed you as my prophet to the nations. —Jeremiah 1:5, NLT

My prayer: Lord God, your design of all of creation is indescribably awe-inspiring. I see and know that you have formed my world, and you have formed me. Body and soul. Just as you want me to be. For your good purposes. Thank you for formulating a plan that included me.

In what particular ways have you been fashioned to contribute to a better world?

Plants/sows

God puts us in a particular place—he plants us right where we need to be—so that we can grow in the way he designed. Likewise, he plants his word in our hearts; it grows within us, so that we can bear much fruit.

> Now the LORD God had planted a garden in the east, in Eden; and there he put the man he had formed. —Genesis 2:8

> Therefore, get rid of all moral filth and the evil that is so prevalent and humbly accept the word planted in you, which can save you. —James 1:21

My prayer: My loving Lord, thank you for your tender care as I have struggled as a tender shoot to push my head above ground and into your light. Because you have planted the seed of your word in my heart and you have been nurturing that seed, it is my joy to bear fruit for you.

What people had a hand in planting God's word in your heart? How has that seed been nurtured?

Establishes

God has built a firm foundation for his kingdom, including setting up the perfect, intricate organization of nature and the rules that govern it. With his unalterable plan for Jesus to reign forever, he has established everything we need for all eternity.

> I will establish my covenant as an everlasting covenant between me and you and your descendants after you for the generations to come, to be your God and the God of your descendants after you. —Genesis 17:7

> Your faithfulness continues through all generations; you established the earth, and it endures. —Psalm 119:90

My prayer: My God, Father, Creator, you not only created the world, you established Jesus as the Rock, and only through him can I be with you. In him, you set forth a new covenant. Through him, you instituted your law and built a foundation of your love in my heart. I am now so blessed to know that your word will endure forever, and on that Rock I stand.

What spiritual habits have you established that are helping to build your knowledge and love of God?

Orders our steps/guides

When we ask him, God shows us the way. He helps us plan what to do or say, influencing our thoughts or putting information or people in our path to advise us. He guides us in the way that is right and good and in keeping with his purpose.

> The steps of a good man are ordered by the LORD: and he delights in his way. —Psalm 37:23, AKJV

> He guides the humble in what is right and teaches them his way. —Psalm 25:9

> For this God is our God for ever and ever; he will be our guide even to the end. —Psalm 48:1

My prayer: My loving Father, when I was finally ready to trust you and submit to you, my earliest cry to you was "Show me the way." I begged you to order my steps, and you did. Thank you for hearing my cry and for continuing to be my Guide. Even when I step off your good path, you lovingly show me that your way is best.

When do you know that your steps are being guided by God?

Sends

When God calls us to do something, we have an important part to play in his plan. He sends us out into the world—maybe outside of our comfort zone—to do his work, using our talents to communicate his message of love, forgiveness, and salvation.

> For God did not send his Son into the world to condemn the world, but to save the world through him. —John 3:17

> Then I heard the voice of the Lord saying, "Whom shall I send? And who will go for us?" And I said, "Here am I. Send me!" —Isaiah 6:8

My prayer: Father, you sent your Son into this broken world, and he did not cling to equality with you (Philippians 2:6). No, he willingly came to earth to do your work, modeling for us how we should live and whom we should serve. Thank you for sending your Holy Spirit to be with me and strengthen me as you send me out into the world to love and serve you.

When has God sent you outside of your comfort zone to do his work? How did it work out? Did you grow? Did others benefit?

Meets

When we believe, we begin a relationship with God. He makes known his presence with us. Whether we are experiencing joy, trouble, grief, anguish, disappointment, fear, loneliness, or any other emotion, he meets us right where we are.

> [Balaam said to Balak,] "Perhaps the LORD will come to meet with me. Whatever he reveals to me I will tell you." Then he went off to a barren height. God met with him.
> —Numbers 23:3b–4a

> My God in his lovingkindness will meet me; God will let me look triumphantly upon my foes. —Psalm 59:10, NASB 1995

My prayer: Lord, it is a wondrous thing that you want to meet with me, and it is so reassuring that you will supply all of my spiritual and physical needs. Thank you for being with me at all times, from the times of the simple, but awesome, joy of being with you to being together in my times of need.

What do you do to meet people where they are, spiritually or emotionally?

Embraces

When we turn to God, he is happy to receive us; he is ready to give us a warm hug, gladly welcoming us into his family. Then, as we share sweet times with him, we can feel his loving warmth and assurance.

> So he [the prodigal son] returned home to his father. And while he was still a long way off, his father saw him coming. Filled with love and compassion, he ran to his son, embraced him, and kissed him. —Luke 15:20, NLT

> His left arm is under my head, and his right arm embraces me. —Song of Solomon 2:6

My prayer: Lord, I have complete peace knowing that I have a place of assurance and rest, right in your loving embrace. There, I know that I am safe and I am loved unconditionally. I am so thankful that you, even in your complete holiness, can receive me, love me, and embrace me because you see me as without sin. Hallelujah! Jesus made me righteous in your eyes.

What, for you, was a particularly wonderful embrace?

Soothes

When the storms roll through our lives, God soothes us. When we are grieving or in pain, he understands our hearts and knows how to gently, sometimes miraculously, relieve us of discomfort.

> [But instead] I would strengthen *and* encourage you with [the words of] my mouth, and the consolation *and* solace of my lips would soothe your suffering *and* lessen your anguish.
> —Job 16:5, AMPCE

> [God will] provide for those who grieve in Zion—to bestow on them a crown of beauty instead of ashes, the oil of joy instead of mourning, and a garment of praise instead of a spirit of despair. —Isaiah 61:3a

My prayer: Your very presence, Lord, is soothing to my mind and soul. Thank you for your power over things great and small. Nothing is too small for you to care about, and nothing is too big for you to handle.

When storms roll through your life or when you are really hurting, what actions or words of encouragement are able to soothe you?

Feeds/nourishes

God provides every good thing for our physical and spiritual nourishment. When we are fortified like this, we can grow and remain strong to do his work. Because we have everything we need, we can focus on him, and the fruit of our labors can be multiplied.

> You prepare a table before me in the presence of my enemies. You anoint my head with oil; my cup overflows. —Psalm 23:5

> Consider the ravens: They do not sow or reap, they have no storeroom or barn; yet God feeds them. And how much more valuable you are than birds! —Luke 12:24

> The eyes of all look to you; you give them their food in due season. —Psalm 145:15, ESV

My prayer: Lord, I now understand that the table you prepare for me is your word; the Bread of Life is your Son, whose body and blood were sacrificed for me. Your word is truth; it sustains me spiritually. Your ways are ever higher than my mere physical needs. Thank you for nourishing me for the here-and-now as well as in ways that are eternal.

What is your favorite way to take spiritual nourishment? Is it usually when you are alone or in the company of others?

Heals

The Hebrew name *Jehovah Rapha* means The God Who Heals. God knows what kind of restoration we require, whether physical, emotional, or spiritual. We often can see the physical results when he cures a disease or heals a surface wound. He also works miracles of emotional and spiritual healing, restoring peace and purity.

> He said, "If you listen carefully to the LORD your God and do what is right in his eyes, if you pay attention to his commands and keep all his decrees, I will not bring on you any of the diseases I brought on the Egyptians, for I am the LORD, who heals you." —Exodus 15:26
>
> LORD my God, I called to you for help, and you healed me. —Psalm 30:2

My prayer: You have healed me, my Lord and my Savior. On all of my earthly injuries, on the wounds from all of my sins, you have put your healing balm. Thank you for restoring me to a right relationship with you and for transforming me so that I can walk in the way that you have in mind.

In the past year, what kind of healing have you experienced? What additional healing do you need?

Shines

When God looks upon us with favor, he is making his face shine upon us. We feel it. We know it. We close our eyes and take a moment to bask in the welcome warmth. We see his blessings day in and day out, regardless of whether those blessings have been requested by us or not. They are evidence of his abiding love.

> Let your face shine on your servant; save me in your unfailing love. —Psalm 31:16

> Now therefore, O our God, listen to the prayer of your servant and to his pleas for mercy, and for your own sake, O LORD, make your face to shine upon your sanctuary, which is desolate. —Daniel 9:17, ESV

My prayer: Thank you, my God and my King, for looking upon me with favor, for making your brilliant and beautiful face shine into my life. Thank you for your gracious love, for wooing me, for welcoming me into your arms and into your kingdom forever.

Reflect on your unmerited blessings, and take a moment to bask in the warmth as God shines his face upon you.

Allows/permits

God has authority over all things. It is true that he permits us to do certain things, to go in a particular direction, to make our own choices even when those choices sometimes result in difficulties or even hurtful consequences. These teach us important lessons. Yet there are some things he does not permit, and he intervenes in order to protect us.

> The LORD will not allow the righteous to hunger, but He will reject the craving of the wicked. —Proverbs 10:3, NASB 2020
>
> No temptation has overtaken you but such as is common to man; and God is faithful, who will not allow you to be tempted beyond what you are able, but with the temptation will provide the way of escape also, so that you will be able to endure it. —1 Corinthians 10:13, NASB 2020

My prayer: Lord, I am so thankful for your sovereignty over all things, including my life, and that you have a plan for me. Thank you for permitting challenges and difficulties to strengthen me. They bend me so that I grow toward your wise and loving ways.

What challenges or difficulties has God permitted in your life, and how have you been strengthened by them?

Relents

When we are suffering some kind of punishment, we can call out to God. Sometimes, when he knows our heart has learned an important lesson, he is willing to relent, showing us his mercy instead of the harsh discipline we deserve.

> Then the LORD relented and did not bring on his people the disaster he had threatened. —Exodus 32:14

> . . . and if that nation I warned repents of its evil, then I will relent and not inflict on it the disaster I had planned. —Jeremiah 18:8

> He remembered his covenant with them and relented because of his unfailing love. —Psalm 106:45, NLT

My prayer: Lord, when I sin or go off in the wrong direction, you have every right to charge me, to bring calamity on me, but you hear my cries; you see me as one who has been cleansed, and you relent. Thank you for your mercy, for the grace with which you shower me. Because of my sins, I deserve the harshest of treatment, but because of the shed blood of your precious Son, I am forgiven and saved.

What was a specific time when God relented, mercifully deciding not to give you the punishment that you deserved?

Tests

There are times when God tests us to help us grow. He allows us to face challenges that will strengthen us. These trials prove our true character and sometimes show us how much we have yet to learn.

> Fire tests the purity of silver and gold, but the LORD tests the heart. —Proverbs 17:3, NLT

> The LORD tests the righteous and the wicked, and His soul hates one who loves violence. —Psalm 11:5, NASB 2020

> But he knows the way that I take; when he has tested me, I will come forth as gold. —Job 23:10

My prayer: Lord, you know my thoughts, and you know that I fear testing because I do not want to fall short. I want to please you in every way. I pray that, moment by moment, your Holy Spirit will strengthen me, especially during times of testing, and that I will never forget where my help comes from.

What are you doing to prepare you for the inevitable times of testing that will come?

Recompenses

The Hebrew name *El Gmulot* means The God of Recompense. God's justice is right and true. He repays people according to their deeds, rewarding the good and avenging evil. Only the sacrifice of Jesus can cancel out the consequences of our sin. He came to seek and to save.

> Say to those who have an anxious heart, "Be strong; fear not! Behold, your God will come with vengeance, with the recompense of God. He will come and save you." —Isaiah 35:4, ESV

> The LORD recompense your work, and a full reward be given you of the LORD God of Israel, under whose wings you have come to trust. —Ruth 2:12, KJ2000

> . . . for a destroyer has come upon her, upon Babylon; her warriors are taken; their bows are broken in pieces, for the LORD is a God of recompense; he will surely repay.
> —Jeremiah 51:56, ESV

My prayer: Lord God, lovers of justice want to see evil repaid, and you assure us that you will reward the good and the evil appropriately. Mercifully, because of the shed blood of Jesus Christ, you see me as righteous, instead of weighed down—and counted out—by my sin. I humbly and heartily thank you for your perfect justice and amazing grace.

When have you seen evil repaid as a consequence of someone's sin against you?

Champions

We can have no stronger champion than God. He supports us in our battles; he upholds us when we are falling, and he advocates for us, particularly when our goal is a righteous one.

> The LORD will march out like a champion, like a warrior he will stir up his zeal; with a shout he will raise the battle cry and will triumph over his enemies. —Isaiah 42:13

> God's my strong champion; I flick off my enemies like flies. Far better to take refuge in God than trust in people; far better to take refuge in God than trust in celebrities. —Psalm 118:7–9, TM

> But the LORD is with me like a powerful champion; therefore my persecutors will stumble and not prevail. They will be put to great shame because they have failed, an everlasting disgrace that will not be forgotten. —Jeremiah 20:11, NASB 2020

My prayer: My great God, you have been my Champion all of my life. You made me and protected me. Though the battle around me was strong and threatened to take me down, you saved me for your own good purpose. Thank you for defending me with love and zeal.

What person has championed your cause? What was the battle? What risk was involved? What did you gain?

Sacrifices

The sacrifice God made when he sent his Son into this world to atone for our sins is unfathomable. Nothing we give could ever measure up. But we can truly turn our hearts over to him—making our lives living sacrifices, making better choices with our time, talents, and treasure—so that we become a sweet aroma that invites others into God's kingdom as well.

> He is the atoning sacrifice for our sins, and not only for ours but also for the sins of the whole world. —1 John 2:2

> But when Christ had offered for all time a single sacrifice for sins, he sat down at the right hand of God. —Hebrews 10:12, ESV

> . . . [Jesus Christ,] who gave himself for us to redeem us from all wickedness and to purify for himself a people that are his very own, eager to do what is good. —Titus 2:14

My prayer: Lord, you have given, given, given, and you finally had to give your own Son to die for the sins of mankind, including my own. From before my birth, you knew me. You knew that I would need a savior, and you provided one, a perfect sacrifice, for me. Now, help me as I give up my former ways so that I may be more pleasing to you. I know full well that I can never be perfect, but thanks to your sacrifice, I am fully cleansed by my Savior's blood.

What is the largest sacrifice you have ever made for another person or cause?

Frees/liberates

Each of us has some kind of sin to which we have been slaves, something we do not want out in the open to be scrutinized by others. Our loving, merciful God releases us from the darkness, the burden, and the bondage of sin. He liberates us, showing us the beauty and freedom of living in his light.

> The Spirit of the Sovereign LORD is on me, because the LORD has anointed me to proclaim good news to the poor. He has sent me to bind up the brokenhearted, to proclaim freedom for the captives and release from darkness for the prisoners.
> —Isaiah 61:1

> Therefore, there is now no condemnation for those who are in Christ Jesus, because through Christ Jesus the law of the Spirit who gives life has set you free from the law of sin and death.
> —Romans 8:1–2

My prayer: Lord, I came to a time when I knew I had allowed myself to be a captive to sin. I hated myself for my transgressions—actions and attitudes that were not just mistakes or poor choices but downright sins. But when I found you and believed that you loved me enough to wipe away all my sin, I found freedom from accusation as well as protection under your wing. I now have a firm foundation to stand upon, and I have victory. Thank you for liberating me from the enemy's accusations and from the guilt and shame that held me captive.

Think about some sin that at one time held you hostage; you just couldn't shake it. (Maybe it still has power over you.) Now describe complete freedom from that sin. How does it feel?

Engraves/writes

God created a permanent record of his laws and his promise of salvation for his people. He inscribed these important messages on tablets of stone, on our hearts, and on Jesus' pierced hands.

> The tablets were the work of God; the writing was the writing of God, engraved on the tablets. —Exodus 32:16

> "But this is the new covenant I will make with the people of Israel after those days," says the LORD. "I will put my instructions deep within them, and I will write them on their hearts. I will be their God, and they will be my people."
> —Jeremiah 31:33, NLT

> See, I have engraved you on the palms of my hands; your walls are ever before me. —Isaiah 49:16

My prayer: Thank you, Lord, for writing a remarkable love story. You engraved it on my heart, so that I would come to you and love you and give my life to you. Because of your faithfulness and sovereignty, I know how the story ends. And, like the beginning that you created, it is very good; in fact, it is perfect.

What message have you had professionally engraved on a surface? Why was it important enough to have engraved?

Cleanses/washes away

The job of cleansing the soul of even a very good person is an incomprehensible work that can only be done by God. When, in humility, we confess our sins, he forgives us and completely removes the guilt we bear, washing away the shame associated with our sin. What a relief!

> I will cleanse them from all the sin they have committed against
> me and will forgive all their sins of rebellion against me.
> —Jeremiah 33:8

> Wash away all my iniquity and cleanse me from my sin.
> —Psalm 51:2

> As far as the east is from the west, so far has he removed our
> transgressions from us. —Psalm 103:12

My prayer: Beautiful Savior, how good it feels to take a warm shower and cleanse the grime from my body! How infinitely good it is that you have cleansed me from all my sin, that inward grime weighing me down and separating me from you. Thank you for cleansing me, enabling me to stand pure before you.

Remember a time when you were really grimy. How did it feel to have all of the dirt and sweat completely washed away?

Transforms

Starting with our hearts, God changes us thoroughly, tenderizing even the stoniest of hearts. His transforming work improves our character and even our physical appearance. Relieved from the burden of guilt and shame, we have a new beauty because we reflect the power of his love.

> Do not conform to the pattern of this world, but be transformed by the renewing of your mind. Then you will be able to test and approve what God's will is—his good, pleasing and perfect will. —Romans 12:2

> And we all, who with unveiled faces contemplate the Lord's glory, are being transformed into his image with ever-increasing glory, which comes from the Lord, who is the Spirit. —2 Corinthians 3:18

My prayer: Lord, mine has been a vast transformation. You have changed me from the inside out. Instead of being my selfish self, I desire to please you. I desire to live for you. I want others to know you for who you are and for what you have done for me. Is there some transformation yet to come? Yes. And, joyfully, I am all yours as you continue to transform me.

As you have matured, what fundamental change has taken place in your spiritual life?

Accomplishes/completes

God has his good and perfect plan for each of us, and he successfully fulfills it. Each plan requires complex linkages with other people's lives as well as the need for perfect timing in varied circumstances including untold hardships. In spite of all this, he carries his plan through to completion in every person and every situation.

> . . . declaring the end from the beginning and from ancient times things not yet done, saying, "My counsel shall stand, and I will accomplish all my purpose . . . I have spoken, and I will bring it to pass; I have purposed, and I will do it."
> —Isaiah 46:10–11, ESV

> . . . being confident of this, that he who began a good work in you will carry it on to completion until the day of Christ Jesus.
> —Philippians 1:6

My prayer: Lord, I cannot fathom all that you have accomplished in my life and in the lives of others, especially those I love, and I cannot fully take in what you have accomplished on the cross. Thank you for your perfect plan and for determining to complete your purposes, all in your perfect timing.

What is something—large or small—that you have accomplished? Maybe it was recent or long ago. How did it feel to complete the work?

Joyous

Imagine the joy of finally receiving something precious that you have wanted for a long time. God is positively jubilant when we turn our hearts toward him, when we are willing to be in right relationship with him. And we are privileged to share in that joy.

> You have made known to me the path of life; you will fill me with joy in your presence, with eternal pleasures at your right hand. —Psalm 16:11

> Do not grieve, for the joy of the LORD is your strength. —Nehemiah 8:10b

My prayer: Lord, it thrills me to know that you take joy in my transformation, and that you see me as I am as well as my ultimate self. You are the great artist, and I am your masterwork. I'm so glad that you see me as I will be, that you forgive my failures, that you are guiding me in paths of righteousness, and that you continue to love me with the everlasting love that only you can have.

What is something that you waited a long time for, then finally received? How did you express your joy?

Glorious

God's glory is all around us: from the showy rainbow or sunset spreading across the sky to a tiny rainbow in a water droplet hanging from a leaf. His wonders, great and small, evoke feelings of delighted admiration and special recognition of his ever-present splendor.

> The heavens declare the glory of God, and the sky above proclaims his handiwork. —Psalm 19:1, ESV

> Arise, shine, for your light has come, and the glory of the LORD rises upon you. See, darkness covers the earth and thick darkness is over the peoples, but the LORD rises upon you and his glory appears over you. —Isaiah 60:1–2

My prayer: My great God, how can mere words describe your glory? The power and the wonder of you, described in the Bible, are too marvelous to grasp, too lofty to analyze. Yet I know full well that the exhaustive yet superb descriptions represent only a fraction of your splendor and magnificence. Thank you for letting me experience part of your glory every day.

Name something glorious that you have seen, heard, tasted, smelled, or touched. What led up to that experience?

Endures

We can be assured that God, with all of his amazing attributes, will remain forever. His love will endure forever; his mercy will endure forever. And so on. When we believe and are saved to live with him in eternity, our joy will never end.

> For great is his love toward us, and the faithfulness of the LORD endures forever. Praise the LORD. —Psalm 117:2

> The grass withers and the flowers fall, but the word of our God endures forever. —Isaiah 40:8

> I know that everything God does will endure forever; nothing can be added to it and nothing taken from it. God does it so that people will fear him. —Ecclesiastes 3:14

My prayer: Lord, your love, mercy, faithfulness, and righteousness never fail. Your word and your promise will endure forever. Thank you for patiently enduring my transformation. It has taken a long time, I know, but I desire to continue to be transformed in many more ways, large and small.

Are you thankful for something in your life that has been particularly long-lasting? What is it, and why?

Omega

The last letter of the Greek alphabet is *omega*. Figuratively, it indicates God's endlessness. He describes himself as the Alpha and the Omega, as does Jesus. Because God is infinite, as Alpha, nothing came before him, and as Omega, nothing will come after him.

> "I am the Alpha and the Omega," says the Lord God, "who is, and who was, and who is to come, the Almighty." —Revelation 1:8

> I am the Alpha and the Omega, the First and the Last, the Beginning and the End. —Revelation 22:13

> Thus says the LORD, the King of Israel and his Redeemer, the LORD of hosts: "I am the first and I am the last; besides me there is no god." —Isaiah 44:6, ESV

My prayer: Lord, you said, "I am . . . the First and the Last." As a human, I cannot conceive of the beginning or the end. What was before the beginning? What will be after the end? The answer can only be you. You were, are, and will be into infinity. It is, and ever will be, impossible to get to the end of your vastness and your greatness, Lord.

Some people like to have the "last word." How would you like to have yourself described at your memorial service?

One

This is a world of many ("little g") gods. People sacrifice time and treasure for so many things, experiences, and status symbols. These do not love us or protect us. There is only one God, and he is the only one who deserves our sacrifices and is truly the only one we need.

> Hear, O Israel: The LORD our God, the LORD is one.
> —Deuteronomy 6:4

> For you are great and do marvelous deeds; you alone are God.
> —Psalm 86:10

> Then the scribe told him, "Well said, Teacher! You have told the truth that 'God is one, and there is no other besides him.'"
> —Mark 12:32, ISV

My prayer: Yes, Lord, you alone are God. There is none like you. In this world, there is pressure to worship other gods, to focus on things of this world, even seemingly good and practical things like our health, education, or the growth of our savings accounts to handle emergencies. But Lord, you are my God, the center of my life. You are the only God, and I trust in you. Please forgive me when I take my eyes off you. You alone are worthy of my faith and focus.

What things of this world draw your attention away from the one true God?

Triune

The Trinity—the Christian Godhead—is one God who is expressed as three persons: Father, Son, and Holy Spirit. Each is fully God and has one or more roles to which we can try to relate: the Father, who brings us into the world, loves, nurtures, and sustains us; the Son, Jesus, who physically walked the earth as a real man, showed us how to live, sacrificed himself to pay for our sin, and was resurrected to live and reign forever; the Spirit, who is with us at all times and who intercedes for us when we do not have the words to pray what is in our hearts.

> There is one body and one Spirit, just as you were called to one hope when you were called; one Lord, one faith, one baptism; one God and Father of all, who is over all and through all and in all. —Ephesians 4:4–6

> Therefore go and make disciples of all nations, baptizing them in the name of the Father and of the Son and of the Holy Spirit. —Matthew 28:19

My prayer: My God—Father, Son, Holy Spirit, three-in-one—the Bible does not use the word "triune," yet you have explained that you are plural in persons, yet you are one God. While your triune nature is difficult to fathom, each person of your Trinity helps me glimpse something of your combined/complex nature and the ways in which you are integral to my life. Thank you for bringing me into this world, teaching me how to live, providing daily comfort and guidance, and making a place for me in your eternal family.

When you pray, how do you most frequently address God, e.g., "Father," "Jesus," "Holy Spirit," "Lord," "Dear God," or some other name? Why do you think that is your go-to choice of address?

Excellent

Because he is perfect, God performs excellent deeds and exhibits the utmost supremacy in everything he does. It would be entirely appropriate to address him using the royal title of "Your Excellency." He is the King above all kings.

> Let them praise the name of the LORD: for his name alone is
> excellent; his glory is above the earth and heaven.
> —Psalm 148:13, AKJV

> But you are a chosen race, a royal priesthood, a holy nation,
> a people for his own possession, that you may proclaim the
> excellencies of him who called you out of darkness into his
> marvelous light. —1 Peter 2:9, ESV

My prayer: Lord, you are not just exceptionally good, everything about you is excellent. The standard you represent is far above anything I or any human could even think of, much less hope to attain. You are excellent throughout your being, and your mercy, lovingkindness, uprightness, wisdom, and guidance are beyond imagining.

What is there about you that has been called "excellent"? What did you do to achieve your level of excellence in that area?

Trustworthy

Throughout the ages and even today, God's promises have proved true. He is completely deserving of our confident trust. If he said something, we can rely on it.

> In you our fathers trusted; they trusted, and you delivered them. To you they cried and were rescued; in you they trusted and were not put to shame. —Psalm 22:4–5, ESV

> The law of the LORD is perfect, refreshing the soul. The statutes of the LORD are trustworthy, making wise the simple. —Psalm 19:7

> Your kingdom is an everlasting kingdom, and your dominion endures through all generations. The LORD is trustworthy in all he promises and faithful in all he does. —Psalm 145:13

My prayer: Father, the more I know about you, the more I see your word come alive in my life. That is refreshing to me. In this finite and fallen world, there are people to be wary of, and there is much to distrust. But I have complete and utter confidence that I can believe every promise that you have made. You have proven yourself to be trustworthy. I praise you for all this and more.

Is it difficult to trust the Lord in any particular area? If so, what? How can you counteract your tendency to think he might not come through?

Generous

Most human beings do not display a readiness to give much more than is necessary. In contrast, God is open-handed, even lavish. He gives so abundantly, with gifts large and small, that we cannot thank him enough for all he has done.

> You open your hand and satisfy the desires of every living thing. —Psalm 145:16

> If any of you lacks wisdom, you should ask God, who gives generously to all without finding fault, and it will be given to you. —James 1:5

My prayer: My gracious and giving God, thank you for being a perfect model of generosity. You more than satisfy all of my needs; you continue to lavish your love and grace upon me. Thank you for doing much more in my life than I could dream of. I pray that I may not cling to wealth, which is uncertain and ultimately not satisfying, but I pray that I will give you glory by mirroring in some measure your generosity.

Who has been the most generous person you have ever known? In what way(s) did they give?

Audible

In addition to his speaking in the sound of thunder, the roar of waves at the seashore, and other attention-getting forces of nature, God uses words that can be heard. His voice was heard at Jesus' baptism, his transfiguration, and on Palm Sunday. Today, his voice is perceptible, and his intentions can be discerned, especially by those whose hearts are close to his.

> And a voice from heaven said, "This is my Son, whom I love; with him I am well pleased." —Matthew 3:17

> [Peter] was still speaking when, behold, a bright cloud over-shadowed them, and a voice from the cloud said, "This is my beloved Son, with whom I am well pleased; listen to him." —Matthew 17:5, ESV

> [Jesus said,] "Now is my soul troubled. And what shall I say? 'Father, save me from this hour'? But for this purpose I have come to this hour. Father, glorify your name." Then a voice came from heaven: "I have glorified it, and I will glorify it again." —John 12:27–28, ESV

My prayer: Great God, your power is audible in nature's elements, and your voice is discerned more personally and meaningfully through your word and in other ways. I cherish the times when you gently whisper right into my soul. Please help me to be sensitive and hospitable to your voice, so that I may respond and do your will.

In what ways have you ever heard from God? Was it a voice? What happened as a result?

Fresh

In Ecclesiastes 1:9, the Teacher observes, "there is nothing new under the sun." But God, the consummate Creator, can make fresh, new ideas and approaches come to life. Though God is unchanging, he is fresh and refreshing daily, even to those who have known him for a long time.

> Because of the LORD's great love we are not consumed, for his compassions never fail. They are new every morning; great is your faithfulness. —Lamentations 3:22–23

> See, I am doing a new thing! Now it springs up; do you not perceive it? I am making a way in the wilderness and streams in the wasteland. —Isaiah 43:19

My prayer: Heavenly Father, you are fresh to me every day, beautifully powerful and relevant, with new insights each day as I awaken. You nourish me daily with the bread of life. And, as with the Israelites and the manna, I must take action each day, not gathering up and storing, but partaking with thanksgiving and being fruitful for your purpose.

What fresh, new insights have you had recently? In what ways do you keep your mind and heart open to new ideas and approaches?

Gifts

Each of us has been gifted in certain ways, with particular talents and strengths. Nobody has all of the gifts, and the gifts each of us has received help us accomplish his plan. God must be so delighted when we listen to his call to use those gifts for his purposes.

> I wish that all of you were as I am. But each of you has your own gift from God; one has this gift, another has that.
> —1 Corinthians 7:7

> We have different gifts, according to the grace given to each of us. If your gift is prophesying, then prophesy in accordance with your faith; if it is serving, then serve; if it is teaching, then teach; if it is to encourage, then give encouragement; if it is giving, then give generously; if it is to lead, do it diligently; if it is to show mercy, do it cheerfully. —Romans 12:6–8

My prayer: Lord, it has taken me a while to know and better appreciate the gifts that you have given to me. I confess that sometimes I have coveted the gifts of others. Yet you have gifted me uniquely. As you lead me, I am moving forward to best employ those unique gifts to honor you and further your kingdom. Thank you for the special gifts that you have designed just for me.

What are some of the gifts, abilities, or talents that you have been given? How do you—or how can you—use them to serve the Lord?

Quickens

In the old-fashioned sense, to *quicken* means to make alive or to revive. God gave us life in the first place, and he resuscitated us when we were in danger of being completely conquered in this sin-darkened world. Without his touch upon our minds, bodies, and hearts, we would be lost.

> But if the Spirit of him that raised up Jesus from the dead dwell in you, he that raised up Christ from the dead shall also quicken your mortal bodies by his Spirit that dwelleth in you. —Romans 8:11, KJV

> And you hath he quickened, who were dead in trespasses and sins. —Ephesians 2:1, KJV

My prayer: Almighty Father, you breathed the breath of life into my new-born body, and when I was grown and was dead in my sins, you revived me; you gave me new life—eternal life—in your Son, Jesus Christ. Both of these were miracles, and I thank you. Now, in the modern sense, I ask you to quicken my steps, Lord, that I may share your gospel with those who need your word of grace.

All believers were dead in their own trespasses and sins before God rescued and revived us. In what ways is it obvious to you that God has resuscitated you?

Embodies

God's spirit took on flesh, becoming human, when he came to earth as Jesus. This incarnation, or embodiment, allows us to better relate to him and to know that he really understands us because, as a human, he experienced the pain of living in a broken world.

> Philip said, "Lord, show us the Father and that will be enough for us." Jesus answered: " . . . Anyone who has seen me has seen the Father . . . The words I say to you I do not speak on my own authority. Rather, it is the Father, living in me, who is doing his work." —John 14:8–10

> For in Christ all the fullness of the Deity lives in bodily form, and in Christ you have been brought to fullness. He is the head over every power and authority. —Colossians 2:9–10

My prayer: O Lord, the greatest embodiment ever is that of Jesus, God Incarnate. Thank you for his life on earth and for securing salvation for those who will believe. Further, thank you for sending your Holy Spirit to live within me. Please help me to become, to the greatest extent possible, a worthy representative of you.

In what ways are you fortifying your ability to be a worthy representative of God?

Receptive

When we acknowledge his sovereignty, we see that God is so hospitable to us. Because of the cleansing blood of Jesus, God is merciful and welcomes us into his holy presence. He graciously receives our prayers, praises, and requests.

> In the morning, LORD, you hear my voice; in the morning I lay my requests before you and wait expectantly. —Psalm 5:3

> But Jesus called the children to him and said, "Let the little children come to me, and do not hinder them, for the kingdom of God belongs to such as these." —Luke 18:16

My prayer: My gracious God, you are so welcoming; you are receptive to my conversation and my pleas for your help. Thank you for your love, for your receptivity, for not turning me away or putting me off, and instead, making a way—sending Jesus to be the way—to you.

What surprises you about God's receptivity to your prayers, praises, and requests? In what ways are you receptive to God's insights and his leading?

Delights

God takes pleasure in us when we take pleasure in him. He is delighted when we obey him and when we follow hard after him to fulfill his plan. Our loving God is inclined toward us, and he delights in pleasing, blessing, and protecting us.

> I say of the holy people who are in the land, "They are the noble ones in whom is all my delight." —Psalm 16:3

> He brought me out into a spacious place; he rescued me because he delighted in me. —Psalm 18:19

My prayer: Abba, Lover of my soul, before I trusted in you, I didn't realize that you would delight in me. I was thrilled that you would forgive me. Now I see that you had a plan for me. You knew that I would turn my face toward you and give you my heart. Thank you for being inclined toward me even when I was unlovable. Still, with all of my remaining imperfections, you know my heart, so you delight in me. How that blesses me!

What people have you found to be delightful? What did they do that pleased you?

Lifts up

When we are humble, and when we have been brought low, God lifts up our heads, so that we can look toward him. At the beginning of our walk with him, as he teaches us and leads us, he lifts us up out of ugliness and self-centeredness to a place of increasing beauty and joy.

> To the roots of the mountains I sank down; the earth beneath barred me in forever. But you, LORD my God, brought my life up from the pit. —Jonah 2:6

> He lifts the poor from the dust and the needy from the garbage dump. He sets them among princes, placing them in seats of honor. For all the earth is the LORD's, and he has set the world in order. —1 Samuel 2:8, NLT

> The LORD upholds all who fall and lifts up all who are bowed down. —Psalm 145:14

My prayer: Compassionate Lord, at one time I was stumbling around in darkness, but you came to save me, to lift up my eyes to see you, and to encourage my heart to want you. Thank you for lifting me from the place of darkness into your saving light and into relationship with you.

We serve the Lord when we lift up others. What do you do to lift the spirits of people you know or those you encounter?

Knits

God unites people—whether blood relatives or members of his family—with the bonds of love, like interlocking stitches which form a single garment. He connects us with others, so that we support each other and together become something that is much greater, and more beautiful, than the sum of its parts.

> [Paul's goal was] that their hearts may be encouraged, being knit together in love, to reach all the riches of full assurance of understanding and the knowledge of God's mystery, which is Christ. —Colossians 2:2, ESV

> From him [Christ] the whole body, fitted and knit together by every supporting ligament, promotes the growth of the body for building up itself in love by the proper working of each individual part. —Ephesians 4:16, HCSB

My prayer: Lord God, I am thankful that my family is bound together with love. May it be ever so. Thank you, too, for leading me to participate in many groups over the years that were knitted together by you. Each has been a deep and wonderful experience. Only you would bring these particular individuals together, and only you can do the work of binding us together as we have focused on you.

In what group have you been knitted together with others? How did those connections develop?

Clothes

God is the provider of everything we need. For everyday living, God even covers us with clothing. More important, he clothes us in robes of righteousness for our life in heaven with him.

> So the Angel of the Lord spoke to those standing before him, "Take off his filthy clothes!" Then he said to him, "See, I have removed your guilt from you, and I will clothe you with splendid robes." —Zechariah 3:4, HCSB

> I delight greatly in the Lord; my soul rejoices in my God. For he has clothed me with garments of salvation and arrayed me in a robe of his righteousness, as a bridegroom adorns his head like a priest, and as a bride adorns herself with her jewels. —Isaiah 61:10

> But the father [of the prodigal son] said to his servants, "Quick! Bring the best robe and put it on him. Put a ring on his finger and sandals on his feet." —Luke 15:22

My prayer: Loving Father, through the blood of your dear Son, you cleansed me of all unrighteousness and clothed me in garments of salvation. What an array that is! My prodigal ways are over. Thank you for welcoming me home to you, celebrating my return to you, and putting on me the very best robe.

Have you ever put on a suit or an outfit that made you "feel like a million bucks"? What was the occasion?

Security

There are many metaphors for God that speak of the security we have in him: rock, fortress, shield, shepherd, hedge. No matter which of these images we ponder, it demonstrates that in him we are free from danger or threat because God is strong, faithful and true. He holds us close and affords us safety from now into eternity.

> Those who fear the LORD are secure; he will be a refuge for their children. —Proverbs 14:26, NLT

> If my house were not right with God, surely he would not have made with me an everlasting covenant, arranged and secured in every part; surely he would not bring to fruition my salvation and grant me my every desire. —2 Samuel 23:5

> I give them eternal life, and they will never perish, and no one will snatch them out of my hand. My Father, who has given them to me, is greater than all, and no one is able to snatch them out of the Father's hand. —John 10:28–29, ESV

My prayer: Abba, in this world, there is so much to upset us, to make us feel unsteady, but because I believe in your word and your promises, I feel secure. I know that you are protecting me even now from all evil and into eternity where you hold my place in your kingdom. Thank you for this tremendous freedom from fear.

What is your favorite metaphor for God that communicates security? Why do you like that particular metaphor?

Releases

One blessing from God that is often unrecognized is protection from the knowledge of our future. Only he knows what is in store for us tomorrow, the next day, and in the years ahead. In his great mercy he releases our future to us moment by moment, day by day. If we could see what is ahead, that would likely be too great a burden for us.

> Don't brag about tomorrow, since you don't know what the day will bring. —Proverbs 27:1, NLT

> Look here, you who say, "Today or tomorrow we are going to a certain town and will stay there a year. We will do business there and make a profit." How do you know what your life will be like tomorrow? Your life is like the morning fog—it's here a little while, then it's gone. —James 4:13–14, NLT

> Therefore do not worry about tomorrow, for tomorrow will worry about itself. Each day has enough trouble of its own. —Matthew 6:34

My prayer: Lord, one of my many sins is that I get ahead of myself and ahead of you. Like the other sheep, I am prone to go my own way, moving toward what looks like better pasture. Please help me trust you and stay right in step with you, God, as you release my future to me day by day.

Although it is tempting—and sometimes fun—to speculate, it is good not to know the future. What is one example of something that was good not to know until it was the right time?

Preserves

Because he loves us, God maintains us and protects us from many of life's misfortunes. He cares for us, preserving us for each day so that we may bear fruit according to his plan.

> The LORD protects and preserves them—they are counted
> among the blessed in the land—he does not give them over to
> the desire of their foes. —Psalm 41:2

> But the LORD made the earth by his power, and he preserves it
> by his wisdom. With his own understanding he stretched out
> the heavens. —Jeremiah 10:12, NLT

My prayer: Father, you created a perfect world, and you are at work preserving and caring for that which is holy in your sight. I, even I, am holy in your sight because of the covering of the righteousness of your Son. Thank you for blessing me in such a radical way, preserving me as your own.

In what way or ways has God preserved you? For what reasons do you think he has done that?

Spares

Instead of punishing us for our sins, God spares us. In justice, he could take our lives, but in mercy he refrains. We are granted yet another chance. He also protects us from evil, sparing us its ravages day by day.

> "On the day when I act," says the LORD Almighty, "they will be my treasured possession. I will spare them, just as a father has compassion and spares his son who serves him." —Malachi 3:17

> Indeed he was ill, and almost died. But God had mercy on him, and not on him only but also on me, to spare me sorrow upon sorrow. —Philippians 2:27

My prayer: Lord, I am amazed at how you look upon me with such love that you spare the just punishment for my many sins. I know, too, that you spare me sorrow upon sorrow. I praise and thank you for looking at me in light of my Savior, Jesus Christ, and for remembering my sins no more.

In what ways have you been spared from the consequences of your sin?

Approves

When we love God, we want his approval. In turn, we do not merely listen to his word, we obey his commands. When we dedicate ourselves to God, making him our focus, we become living sacrifices. God approves and is pleased by these love offerings.

> On the contrary, we speak as those approved by God to be entrusted with the gospel. We are not trying to please people but God, who tests our hearts. —1 Thessalonians 2:4

> No doubt there have to be differences among you to show which of you have God's approval. —1 Corinthians 11:19

My prayer: Thank you, Lord, for the cloak of righteousness in Jesus Christ that completely covers me. For without it, I know that I could not win your approval. Your approval means everything to me. Thank you for your great sacrifice through Jesus, demonstrating love, humility, obedience, and trust.

Considering your love offerings, of which do you think God particularly approves?

Favors

When we consider the many benefits provided by God, it is difficult to comprehend the vast extent of his grace and mercy toward us. We are, indeed, blessed and highly favored by God because of the sacrificial work of Jesus Christ on our behalf.

> For his anger lasts only a moment, but his favor lasts a lifetime; weeping may stay for the night, but rejoicing comes in the morning. —Psalm 30:5

> For he says, "In the time of my favor I heard you, and in the day of salvation I helped you." I tell you, now is the time of God's favor, now is the day of salvation. —2 Corinthians 6:2

My prayer: Lord, I am sure I do not know the depth of your favor, all of the intervention that you have made on my behalf. But I do know that your favor rests on me through the precious blood of Christ my Savior. Thank you for this covering of salvation and special blessings.

Have you ever felt that you had favored status (e.g., receiving special benefits, someone treating you as a favorite) in your personal or professional life? If so, how did you attain that status?

Banner

One of the Hebrew names for God is *Jehovah Nissi*, meaning The LORD Is My Banner. When the name was ascribed to God long ago, having a banner as a conspicuous rallying point was important in wartime. Likewise today, we need a rallying point. We must follow God's lead in order to win the battle. Therefore we, too, can embrace calling him our banner.

> Moses built an altar and called it The LORD is my Banner.
> —Exodus 17:15

> This is what the Sovereign LORD says: "See, I will beckon to the nations, I will lift up my banner to the peoples; they will bring your sons in their arms and carry your daughters on their hips." —Isaiah 49:22

My prayer: O Lord, my Banner, you are my rallying point; I look to you to lead me. You are not just a symbol of love, you also provide all that I need as I face the world. Love can win—will win—when it is the kind of love that you have shown to us, as exemplified in Jesus Christ.

The children's song "His Banner Over Me Is Love" is a sweet reminder of our Lord's proclamation of our importance. As an adult, how does it help you to remember that his banner over you is love?

Drives out

God is able to completely dispel our enemy. This even includes forcing away negative thoughts that can plague us: thoughts of guilt, inadequacy, or unworthiness. God helps us see ourselves in light of our new identity in him, so that we can stand strong.

> Little by little I will drive them out before you, until you have
> increased enough to take possession of the land.
> —Exodus 23:30

> The eternal God is your refuge, and underneath are the everlasting arms. He will drive out your enemies before you, saying,
> "Destroy them!" —Deuteronomy 33:27

My prayer: Wise and powerful Lord, I see how you have driven the enemy out of my life little by little. The enemy is crafty, I know, and he is seeking a foothold. He will not win because you continue to be my Refuge and my Strength. You hold me by my right hand. Thank you, Lord.

God's desire is for you to live into your new identity in him, with complete freedom from any negative thoughts of guilt, inadequacy, or unworthiness. In what ways do you remember to call on him to drive away these thoughts?

Humbles

At times we pump ourselves up, and we can feel pretty full of ourselves. God knows how to test us and take us down a peg or two (or more), to reestablish our focus on him. Yes, our dignity may be bruised, but our priorities are restored.

> Remember how the LORD your God led you all the way in the wilderness these forty years, to humble and test you in order to know what was in your heart, whether or not you would keep his commands. —Deuteronomy 8:2

> God, who is enthroned from of old, who does not change—he will hear them and humble them, because they have no fear of God. —Psalm 55:19

My prayer: Lord, I confess that many times I am not at all humble. Sometimes I look to others to lift me up, or in some way I lift myself up, because I feel the need for affirmation. I pray that your Holy Spirit will come alongside and gently remind me of my place in this world, so that I will remember that only you are worthy of praise.

Have you ever felt humbled in the presence of a particular person? Who was it, and what were the circumstances?

Quiets/calms

God has a beautiful way of calming our spirits. When we are distressed or in a panic, we run to him, and he quiets our hearts. When we ask for peace, he gives us exactly what we need.

> The LORD your God is in your midst, a mighty one who will save; he will rejoice over you with gladness; he will quiet you by his love; he will exult over you with loud singing.
> —Zephaniah 3:17, ESV

> You quieted the raging oceans with their pounding waves and silenced the shouting of the nations. —Psalm 65:7, NLT

> For I am the Lord your God, who makes the sea calm when its waves are thundering: the Lord of armies is his name.
> —Isaiah 51:15, BBE

My prayer: Loving and all-powerful God, when my heart is roaring, you quiet me down. You cause me to lift my face to you so that I will look to you and ask for your unfailing help. You quiet my heart when I redirect my focus to you. Thank you for demonstrating your love for me in this way.

What is an example of a time when you needed God to quiet your heart?

Purifies

Having contaminants removed from our lives can be painful. When God purges out the bad stuff, he makes room for the good. The ongoing results of our purification are pleasing to God and attractive to others. When others observe the change in us, they are witness to our living testimony.

> Many will be purified, made spotless and refined, but the wicked will continue to be wicked. None of the wicked will understand, but those who are wise will understand. —Daniel 12:10

> Then I will purify the lips of the peoples, that all of them may call on the name of the Lord and serve him shoulder to shoulder. —Zephaniah 3:9

My prayer: My Deliverer, the purification process is a serious thing, difficult, and often disheartening. Lord, you have been gentle with me as you have been refining me (and not finished yet). You know just how to chasten my spirit without crushing it. Thank you for your love and tender mercy as you soften and purify my heart and renew a right spirit within me.

Has anyone ever commented on a change in you? In what ways has the Lord been working on purifying your heart or refining you?

Receives

No one has given more than God; he is the Supreme Giver. God also receives. He receives our praise and the glory due his name. He receives our confessions and our requests, and he responds in the perfect way. And he receives us into his presence. He welcomes us and allows us to come in.

> And since God receives glory because of the Son, he will give
> his own glory to the Son, and he will do so at once.
> —John 13:32, NLT

> If I go and prepare a place for you, I will come again and
> receive you to Myself, that where I am, there you may be also.
> —John 14:3, NASB 1995

My prayer: You, Lord, are so worthy of receiving (glory, honor, thanks, trust, and more), but your word indicates that your people do most of the receiving. We have received the Holy Spirit, mercy, salvation, comfort, sight, healing, protection, forgiveness, strength, power, and so much more. You daily demonstrate that giving is part of your character. Thank you for your abundant gifts as well as for receiving me into your kingdom.

What kinds of things has the Lord received from you? What is your favorite thing to give him?

Soon-coming/returning

God in Jesus is called the soon-coming King. For almost two thousand years, people have looked forward to his promised return. But God's timing is not our timing. Although Jesus' return has not happened yet, we can await his return with confidence. God has promised, and he will be faithful to fulfill his promise.

> So you also must be ready, because the Son of Man will come at an hour when you do not expect him. —Matthew 24:44

> But this will happen to each in the right order—Christ having been the first to rise, and afterwards Christ's people rising at his return. —1 Corinthians 15:23, WEY

> For the Lord himself will descend from heaven with a cry of command, with the voice of an archangel, and with the sound of the trumpet of God. And the dead in Christ will rise first. —1 Thessalonians 4:16, ESV

My prayer: Lord, no human knows the time when you will return to the earth. Your word (2 Peter 3:8) tells us that with you "one day is like a thousand years and a thousand years are like a day." Your timing and your conception of time, though not the same as mine, are perfect. So, when I describe you as "soon-coming," it is true. I trust you, and I wait in eager anticipation for Jesus' return which is near at hand.

What are you doing that expresses your readiness for Christ's imminent return?

Worthy (of glory, honor, thanks)

Because of his character, because of everything he is, because of all he has accomplished and still will accomplish, God is deserving of all glory and honor. He is so worthy of all the thanksgiving we can possibly show him.

> You are worthy, our Lord and God, to receive glory and honor and power, for you created all things, and by your will they were created and have their being. —Revelation 4:11

> In a loud voice they were saying: "Worthy is the Lamb, who was slain, to receive power and wealth and wisdom and strength and honor and glory and praise!" —Revelation 5:12

My prayer: Yahweh, only you are worthy. I was not worthy to have you come into my life, but because of your great love and the saving blood of Jesus Christ, you have allowed me—indeed, invited me—to be in your presence. You saved me; you healed me, because you love me. And you are worthy of all of my thanks and praise.

In what ways do you express glory, honor, and thanks to God for who he is?

Welcomes

Who could imagine the Creator and King of the universe joyously greeting us when we arrive at the gates of his eternal kingdom? Because God is our Abba, he will be glad to warmly, lovingly welcome us to our forever home.

> . . . and you will receive a rich welcome into the eternal kingdom of our Lord and Savior Jesus Christ. —2 Peter 1:11

> . . . but the crowds learned about it and followed him. He welcomed them and spoke to them about the kingdom of God, and healed those who needed healing. —Luke 9:11

My prayer: Lord, thank you for welcoming me into your family. I can anticipate a joyous welcome into your eternal kingdom as well. You are a promise keeper, and when it is my time to leave my earthly home—as you have predetermined—I will appear before you, covered in the righteousness of Christ my Savior, and I will experience the completion of your promise.

In what ways do you welcome others into your home or into your circle of friends?

Unique

God is truly unlike anyone we have ever met or anything we have ever known. He is the only one with perfect character, the only one who could have performed his marvelous works, and the only one who knows and loves in dimensions far beyond our comprehension.

> "To whom will you compare me? Or who is my equal?" says the Holy One. —Isaiah 40:25

> I am the LORD, and there is no other; apart from me there is no God. I will strengthen you, though you have not acknowledged me, so that from the rising of the sun to the place of its setting people may know there is none besides me. I am the LORD, and there is no other. —Isaiah 45:5–6

My prayer: Yahweh, only you are God. Only you, out of timelessness, could have created this universe (and even other universes that have been theorized by physicists throughout the centuries). Only you could have set the universe into motion, fine-tuning everything to hold together in a unique way. Only you could have conceptualized and put into action the one, particular way for me to come into your holy presence, through my Lord and Savior Jesus Christ. I am in awe of you.

As you consider some of the myriad ways in which God is unparalleled, what is your favorite aspect of the uniqueness of God?

Living

God is not just an ideal, nor is he a concept, a symbol, or "the Universe," and he is certainly not an inanimate idol. He is living, an actual presence who is with us. We can feel him with us; we can speak to him, and he answers us.

> But the LORD is the true God; he is the living God, the eternal King. When he is angry, the earth trembles; the nations cannot endure his wrath. —Jeremiah 10:10

> That is why we labor and strive, because we have put our hope in the living God, who is the Savior of all people, and especially of those who believe. —1 Timothy 4:10

My prayer: Lord, the gravity of having a relationship with you—Almighty and Living God—overwhelms me. You are not some representation of a power or an idea. You are the great God who was and is and is to come. Yet you, my Living God, have invited me into a vibrant relationship with you, and you participate in that relationship. You show me daily that you live and are present with me. I praise you for your invitation and for leading me as I engage in the work of your vast and wonderful plan.

What are a couple of examples in which God showed you that he is alive and active, in addition to being the standard of goodness, power, and love?

True

Our God is the one true God, not a false promise nor a man-made notion. He daily proves that he is faithful to his word, and he is able to make what seems impossible come to fruition. Nothing about him is inconsistent. His character is flawless.

> Now this is eternal life: that they know you, the only true God, and Jesus Christ, whom you have sent. —John 17:3

> We know also that the Son of God has come and has given us understanding, so that we may know him who is true. And we are in him who is true by being in his Son Jesus Christ. He is the true God and eternal life. —1 John 5:20

My prayer: Lord God, you are the only way to everlasting life; you are the original, authentic, True North, my bearing. True to your word, you will bring about the hoped-for result which is eternal life with you. Your Son *is* the Promised One. Through him, the truth of your love is, and will be, reality for all eternity.

Who is the truest person you have ever known (i.e., true to themselves, true to their cause, true to their word)? Was it easy or hard to be around them?

Steadfast

More dedicated than the most faithful person we know or have ever heard of, God is resolutely firm and unwavering in his love for us. Loyal, committed, constant, and solid, he never fails us.

> For the LORD is good; his steadfast love endures forever, and his faithfulness to all generations. —Psalm 100:5, ESV

> . . . and [Solomon] said, "O LORD, God of Israel, there is no God like you, in heaven above or on earth beneath, keeping covenant and showing steadfast love to your servants who walk before you with all their heart." —1 Kings 8:23, ESV

My prayer: My Lord, your word repeatedly refers to your love as steadfast, and this description is often coupled with faithfulness. This means I can trust that you will, indeed, never leave me nor forsake me, that you will always love me, and that you have your best in mind for me. You model the perfect example of what it means to love: steadfastly, enduring through all generations.

In our culture, many people find it difficult to remain steadfast. In what way(s) have you been particularly steadfast?

Irresistible

If we are able to glimpse God's character and receive the testimonies of his marvelous works, his truth is too attractive to reject. Those whose hearts are not completely hardened can see that the case for God is too powerful, too convincing to be resisted.

> One of you will say to me: "Then why does God still blame us? For who is able to resist his will?" —Romans 9:19

> All those the Father gives me will come to me, and whoever comes to me I will never drive away. —John 6:37

> One of those listening was a woman from the city of Thyatira named Lydia, a dealer in purple cloth. She was a worshiper of God. The Lord opened her heart to respond to Paul's message. —Acts 16:14

My prayer: My Lord, some people do reject you. If they are not willing to come to you, their hearts must be too hard. Ultimately, to their dismay, they will find that their attitudes and deeds have ensnared them and that their rejection of you could only lead to your banishment of them. Thank you for softening my heart, for surrounding me with your love and grace, and for making yourself irresistible to me. By your character and through your will, you have drawn me to yourself. Lord God, I cherish the closeness we share.

Have you found God's message of love and salvation to be irresistible? If so, when and how did that occur?

Evident

Evidence of God is everywhere: in the wonders of nature, in the miracle of every baby's birth, in the obviousness of answered prayer. In these things and in so much more, there is God, making his works apparent for all to see.

> For the wrath of God is revealed from heaven against all ungodliness and unrighteousness of people who suppress the truth in unrighteousness, because that which is known about God is evident within them; for God made it evident to them. —Romans 1:18–19, NASB 2020

> Yet he has not left himself without testimony: He has shown kindness by giving you rain from heaven and crops in their seasons; he provides you with plenty of food and fills your hearts with joy. —Acts 14:17

> God did this [made all nations from one man] so that they would seek him and perhaps reach out for him and find him, though he is not far from any one of us. —Acts 17:27

My prayer: Lord, my mind is boggled when I consider all of the evidence of your existence and proof of your love that you place right in front of me every day. When faced with such a weight of evidence, who can deny you? Thank you for making yourself and your love so noticeable to me.

What do you consider to be obvious evidence of God's existence?

Vital

Absolutely indispensable for the continuation of our world, God is vital to life. He graciously provides everything that we need to live, and he goes beyond the basics as he directs us to think about what is true, noble, right, pure, lovely, admirable, and excellent (Philippians 4:8). When we contemplate these things, our deeds will follow.

> He humbled you, causing you to hunger and then feeding you
> with manna, which neither you nor your ancestors had known,
> to teach you that man does not live on bread alone but on
> every word that comes from the mouth of the LORD.
> —Deuteronomy 8:3

> Unless the LORD builds a house, the work of the builders is
> wasted. Unless the LORD protects a city, guarding it with sentries will do no good. —Psalm 127:1, NLT

> For in him we live and move and exist. As some of your own
> poets have said, "We are his offspring." —Acts 17:28, NLT

My prayer: Lord, the precise word *vital* is not in the Bible as a way of describing you, and yet I honor you this day by acknowledging that you are absolutely necessary. Vital. Without you, there is no hope, nothing worthwhile. You are essential to me and to everything in all of eternity past and eternity future. You feed, sustain, protect, and offer a future to those who love you. Without a relationship with you, I have nothing and am nothing.

In what ways is God vital to you? How does that help you as you grow in your relationship with him and in your testimony to others?

Anoints

When we give our heart to him, God confers on each of us his blessing and anoints us by filling us with the Holy Spirit. The Holy Spirit empowers us to do things to accomplish God's purposes. Having received special blessings like wisdom, understanding, fortitude, or other gifts, we dedicate our lives in service to God.

> You love righteousness and hate wickedness; therefore God, your God, has set you above your companions by anointing you with the oil of joy. —Psalm 45:7

> As for you, the anointing you received from him remains in you, and you do not need anyone to teach you. But as his anointing teaches you about all things and as that anointing is real, not counterfeit—just as it has taught you, remain in him. —1 John 2:27

My prayer: Lord, I have not really thought of myself as "anointed," but now I see that you have anointed me by filling me with the Holy Spirit who empowers me to do your will. You have set me apart for you, protecting me throughout the years. Thank you for calling me to serve you and for empowering me to do it in a way that will fulfill your purposes.

What special blessing or anointing have you received? And how do you use it to do the Lord's work, doing good, lifting people up, or performing other special tasks?

Adopts

In earthly adoptions, the children usually do not get to choose their new parents. However, in spiritual adoptions—when we become Christians—we (the children) choose to accept God as our Father, and he lovingly agrees to take us on as his own. In all of these circumstances, there is much joy in heaven and on earth.

> Yet to all who did receive him, to those who believed in his name, he gave the right to become children of God—children born not of natural descent, nor of human decision or a husband's will, but born of God. —John 1:12–13

> But when the fullness of the time came, God sent forth his Son, born of a woman, born under the Law, so that he might redeem those who were under the Law, that we might receive the adoption as sons and daughters. —Galatians 4:4–5, NASB 2020

My prayer: Lord, you blessed me so much when you gave me my wonderful earthly mother and father. And now, I am infinitely more blessed to have you as my heavenly Father here on earth and in heaven throughout eternity. I praise you for adopting me into your forever family.

When did you understand that you had been adopted into God's beloved family?

Rock

The rock is such an apt symbol for God, who in ancient days was called the Rock of Israel. This represents his permanence, strength, and security. In him, people who are in danger take refuge.

> But the LORD has become my fortress, and my God the rock in whom I take refuge. —Psalm 94:22

> They remembered that God was their Rock, that God Most High was their Redeemer. —Psalm 78:35

My prayer: O God, you are my Rock, my Strength. Your attributes are solid and unchanging. I know that I can run to you for security, and you will always protect me. I am confident in your word, and I fully know that I can stand upon the firm foundation that you have provided.

In what ways do you consider God to be your Rock? What does that description mean to you?

Thoughtful

God is not only mindful—aware—of us, he thinks seriously about his world and shows care and consideration in the way he treats his people. His thoughtfulness is shown in his works, in the myriad ways in which he has blessed us.

> You have multiplied, O LORD my God, your wondrous deeds and your thoughts toward us; none can compare with you! I will proclaim and tell of them, yet they are more than can be told. —Psalm 40:5, ESV

> How great are your works, O LORD! Your thoughts are very deep! —Psalm 92:5, ESV

My prayer: Lord, because you know all things, you have abundantly, thoughtfully, given me everything I need and more. Your word. Your very self. I praise you for your thoughtful consideration in the way that you have made me and in the perfect way you opened the door wide for me to rush to you.

In what ways do you express your thoughtfulness to others?

Mine

God is mine. He is yours, too. And each of us belongs to him. Each of us has our own unique, personal relationship with God, walking with him, listening to him, learning from him, being transformed by him. It is wonderful that sharing him with others does not diminish our portion. Instead, sharing him actually grows our own treasure as we develop greater unity.

> I will give them a heart to know me, that I am the LORD. They will be my people, and I will be their God, for they will return to me with all their heart. —Jeremiah 24:7

> O God, you are my God; earnestly I seek you; my soul thirsts for you; my flesh faints for you, as in a dry and weary land where there is no water. —Psalm 63:1, ESV

> My beloved is mine and I am his. —Song of Solomon 2:16a

My prayer: Lord, you are my Rock and my Fortress, my Deliverer, my Redeemer, my Helper, my Guide, and the Lover of my soul. Our relationship is deep and personal. Everything about you is extraordinary, and now, as your heir, I can claim you as my heavenly Father. I am so thankful that you are mine and I am yours.

When did you first hear about having a personal relationship with God or Jesus (accepting him as your own), and how did you respond to that concept?

Encourages

Instead of harsh treatment, God more often gives us the support, confidence, and hope we need to continue to trust in him and to walk in his ways. His encouragement provides the physical, emotional, and spiritual strength we require, no matter what.

> [Jesus said,] "I have told you these things, so that in me you may have peace. In this world you will have trouble. But take heart! I have overcome the world." —John 16:33

> May the God who gives endurance and encouragement give you the same attitude of mind toward each other that Christ Jesus had. —Romans 15:5

My prayer: Faithful and loving Lord, you know everything about me. You know my situation; you know every detail about the way you designed me, and you know what your plan is for me. You encourage me when I am feeling down, troubled, or "less than." Thank you for your comfort, for your promises, and for the truth of who you are.

At what times do you most need encouragement? Who is your biggest encourager?

Blesses

God has lavishly conferred prosperity and happiness on us in countless ways. We recognize that he has already blessed us, physically, spiritually, and relationally. And, perfect in lovingkindness, he steps in and shows us additional favor.

> Give generously to them and do so without a grudging heart;
> then because of this the LORD your God will bless you in all
> your work and in everything you put your hand to.
> —Deuteronomy 15:10

> May God be gracious to us and bless us and make his face
> shine on us—so that your ways may be known on earth, your
> salvation among all nations. —Psalm 67:1b–2

> From this day on, I will bless you. —Haggai 2:19b

My prayer: All-giving Father, oh, how you have blessed me! I cannot thank you enough for all that you have so generously provided. I know that you care deeply for me and have protected me all along my journey, adding blessing upon blessing. I worship you for the richness of your goodness, mercy, and love.

When you count your blessings, what things top your list?

Sweet

Sweet is descriptive of God's decrees and his word. Moreover, he shows us the sweetness of fellowship, so that we want to draw nearer to him. All of these enable us to deepen our relationship with him and grow in our obedience and faith.

> Taste and see that the LORD is good; blessed is the one who takes refuge in him. —Psalm 34:8

> The fear of the LORD is pure, enduring forever. The decrees of the LORD are firm, and all of them are righteous. They are more precious than gold, than much pure gold; they are sweeter than honey, than honey from the honeycomb. —Psalm 19:9–10

> How sweet are your words to my taste, sweeter than honey to my mouth! —Psalm 119:103

My prayer: Kind and loving Father, you have nurtured me so steadily. I do taste and see your goodness, and I know that your decrees are upright and true. I delight in the sweet taste of your word, which is no longer just milk to me but solid food. Thank you, my Lord, for helping me avoid the bitterness that can come from willful disobedience and for helping me recognize the sweetness of this time in my earthly life.

What is the sweetest aspect of your relationship with God? What about his word do you consider to be delicious?

Song

Our hearts are filled with musical, even poetic, expressions about God that penetrate our very being. Like a song, the joy of God's presence carries us along in sweet connection with him. Praise songs allow us to meditate on every aspect of him, and the lyrics reside deep within our souls, for he is our beloved.

> The LORD is my strength and song, And he has become my salvation. This is my God, and I will praise him, My father's God, and I will exalt him. —Exodus 15:2, NASB 2020

> See, God has come to save me. I will trust in him and not be afraid. The LORD God is my strength and my song; he has given me victory. —Isaiah 12:2, NLT

My prayer: Lord, to speak of you in such a limited way, as a "song," is not to diminish your greatness. No, when I call you "my Song," I acknowledge and praise you as my inspiration. Everything about you wells up and gives me strength. As "my Song" you reside in the tenderest parts of my heart. In fact, you fill my heart with "songs of deliverance" and praise. Like a song, a wonderful love song, you are in my heart always, sweetly, deeply.

Do you ever awaken with a song of praise on your mind? What songs fill your heart with praise?

Reassures

When we have doubts and fears, God provides just the right words in Scripture, a recollection of his past faithfulness, or people in our lives to help us stop worrying. When we trust that he is in control and has our best in mind, we find strength.

> So do not fear, for I am with you; do not be dismayed, for I am your God. I will strengthen you and help you; I will uphold you with my righteous right hand. —Isaiah 41:10

> What, then, shall we say in response to these things? If God is for us, who can be against us? —Romans 8:31

> When doubts filled my mind, your comfort gave me renewed hope and cheer. —Psalm 94:19, NLT

My prayer: Lord, as I read about your goodness and faithfulness, and then as I witness and experience the same, it is all the reassurance I need. I know and believe that because you love me, I need not fear. Thank you for the reassurances in your word and for proving true to your promises, time and again.

What acts of God's faithfulness do you recall to give you reassurance when you have doubts or fears? Have you memorized a particular Bible verse that provides reassurance when the need arises?

Examines

Although God knows all, we can be certain that he inspects us in detail to determine the true condition of our hearts. He judges whether or not we believe him and seek to do his will. To ensure that his justice is served and his righteousness prevails, he sees comprehensively into every situation.

> I the LORD search the heart and examine the mind, to reward each person according to their conduct, according to what their deeds deserve. —Jeremiah 17:10

> Though you probe my heart, though you examine me at night and test me, you will find that I have planned no evil; my mouth has not transgressed. —Psalm 17:3

My prayer: Lord, you know my thoughts and my ways. You examine me, and you would find me wanting, but for the blood of my Savior, Jesus Christ. Thank you for continually purifying me. Although I know that I fall short, you still are doing a work in me. It is truly the desire of my heart to be pleasing to you at all times.

How does thinking about God examining your heart in detail change your attitude or behavior?

Vindicates

When we ally ourselves with God, some people may criticize or even attack us. Their judgment does not matter. When we have committed to follow Jesus, God moves us from the state of injustice to justice. He has our back. He defends us and clears us from accusations or unfair charges, so that we emerge unscathed.

> I cry out to God Most High, to God, who vindicates me.
> —Psalm 57:2

> He who vindicates me is near. Who then will bring charges against me? Let us face each other! Who is my accuser? Let him confront me! It is the Sovereign LORD who helps me.
> —Isaiah 50:8–9a

> ". . . no weapon forged against you will prevail, and you will refute every tongue that accuses you. This is the heritage of the servants of the LORD, and this is their vindication from me," declares the LORD. —Isaiah 54:17

My prayer: Gracious Protector, I believe that by the power of Jesus, you have removed from me all accusation, whether the accusation is true or not. Thank you! You have delivered me from the blaming, shaming arrows of the evil one, and you have ushered me into your peace.

Have you ever been unjustly accused, even in a small matter? Assuming you were cleared of the accusation, how did it feel to be proven right?

Forgives

Because of his overwhelming love and mercy, God does not remain angry at us for our offenses. Instead of remaining angry, he forgives us, canceling our debt to him and relieving the full punishment that we deserve.

> Who is a God like you, who pardons sin and forgives the transgression of the remnant of his inheritance? You do not stay angry forever but delight to show mercy. —Micah 7:18

> Get rid of all bitterness, rage and anger, brawling and slander, along with every form of malice. Be kind and compassionate to one another, forgiving each other, just as in Christ God forgave you. —Ephesians 4:31–32

My prayer: Merciful Father, how hard it is for me to forgive sometimes, and yet you have demonstrated for me the full measure of forgiveness. When I did not deserve anything but condemnation and death, you sent your Son to die as payment for my sins, past, present and future. This is stunning. Thank you for your great, great mercy in granting me complete forgiveness.

What was something that was hard for you to forgive? Were you able to? If so, how did you bring yourself to do so?

Heroic

We know that God is all-powerful and can do anything, yet it seems we don't often admire him for being heroic. Since the beginning of time, he has accomplished great things through bold acts, and his character is extraordinarily, perfectly noble. All of history has witnessed his heroism.

> Generation to generation they will tell your works and they will show your heroism! —Psalm 145:4, ABPE

> He is the God who avenges me, who subdues nations under me, who saves me from my enemies. You exalted me above my foes; from a violent man you rescued me. —Psalm 18:47–48

My prayer: Lord, calling you "heroic" does not speak highly enough of your astounding might and your unquestionable sovereignty. As I consider all that you have done for me, it is so right to call you my hero. In the person of Jesus Christ, you literally died to save me. What a wonder!

Have you regarded any particular person as your hero or heroine? Who was it, and why did you consider them to be heroic?

Savior

Our world is full of danger, some of which we cannot even see. But God protects us day by day from the evils around us and rescues us at just the right time because he loves us and wants to offer us a beautiful eternity with him.

> Our God is a God who saves; from the Sovereign LORD comes escape from death. —Psalm 68:20

> The LORD their God will save his people on that day as a shepherd saves his flock. They will sparkle in his land like jewels in a crown. —Zechariah 9:16

My prayer: Lord, you chose me; you saved me, even before I recognized how much I needed to be rescued. You are my Light and my Salvation, and I am not afraid of what will happen to me when I pass from this life. I am incredibly blessed to know for certain that when I do pass from the earth, it will be to spend eternity with you. Thank you, my loving Savior, for preserving my life so that I could come to know you in this life and be with you for all time.

Has anyone saved you from injury or death? If so, what was your feeling about that person right at that time?

Redeems

During the time before we accepted God's free gift of salvation, we were held captive to the darkness of sin. We could not be in God's holy presence because of the stench of our sins. But God came to save us from the power of sin and death; he paid the ransom to release us from sin's imprisonment. The price of our redemption was the blood sacrifice of God's own Son, Jesus.

> Praise the LORD, my soul, and forget not all his benefits—who forgives all your sins and heals all your diseases, who redeems your life from the pit and crowns you with love and compassion, who satisfies your desires with good things so that your youth is renewed like the eagle's. —Psalm 103:2–5
>
> But now, this is what the LORD says—he who created you, Jacob, he who formed you, Israel: "Do not fear, for I have redeemed you; I have summoned you by name; you are mine." —Isaiah 43:1

My prayer: Lord, please help me fully accept the gift of grace and redemption that you have freely given me; help me not try to redeem myself. Intellectually, I know that I cannot redeem myself, and my heart sometimes must be reminded that you have already done it all. Thank you, my Lord and my Redeemer.

Think about the precious items in a pawn shop that are waiting to be bought back by their original owners at an exorbitant premium. Now, think about the price that was paid to rescue you from the grasp of sin, and write a prayer of thanks to the God who saved you.

Refines

In a careful, customized process, God removes impurities and unwanted elements from us. Some of the changes are immediate; some take longer; some are drastic; some are subtle. Gradually, lovingly, the great Refiner is getting rid of the dross and disclosing the rare beauty that he knows is within us.

> For you, God, tested us; you refined us like silver.
> —Psalm 66:10

> When I will turn my attention to you, I'll refine your dross as in a furnace. I'll remove all your alloy. —Isaiah 1:25, ISV

My prayer: My Lord, I should be afraid when I ask you to continue to refine me, test me, and purify my heart. Changes are hard. Yet I know that in your wisdom and love, you will do what is best to shape me into the person that you desire me to be. Thank you for fine-tuning me, so that I can be a compelling testament to your love and grace.

What is something unlovely that has been refined out of you as a result of God's loving purification?

Sanctifies

Whether we acknowledge it or not, each of us has been waiting to be lifted up from our mire of self-determination to the purity of God's direction. God sets each of us apart, declaring that we are to be holy, righteous. Cleansed from the stench of sin, we can be in his presence.

> You shall sanctify him, for he offers the bread of your God. He shall be holy to you, for I, the LORD, who sanctify you, am holy. —Leviticus 21:8, ESV

> And that [wrong-doers and deceived] is what some of you were. But you were washed, you were sanctified, you were justified in the name of the Lord Jesus Christ and by the Spirit of our God. —1 Corinthians 6:11

My prayer: Yes, Lord, you can do anything, even sanctify the worst of sinners. Thank you for freeing me from sin, for setting me apart for your good purposes. I know that you have not finished my transformation yet, but you are working in me in a mighty way so that my all of my actions and the desires of my heart conform to Jesus' example.

In what ways has God set you apart, so that you can participate in his accomplishing his plan?

Gives peace

God does not want discord within us nor attacks from the outside. When we focus on him, he creates within us a calm, quiet state of mind. He orders our thoughts. By God's hand and through our obedience to him, discord in our lives can be turned into agreement and harmony.

> The LORD gives strength to his people; the LORD blesses his people with peace. —Psalm 29:11

> Peace I leave with you; my peace I give you. I do not give to you as the world gives. Do not let your hearts be troubled and do not be afraid. —John 14:27

> You will keep in perfect peace those whose minds are steadfast, because they trust in you. —Isaiah 26:3

My prayer: Holy God, thank you for showing me the beauty of peace—peace of mind and heart—as I trust and rest in you. Before you lived in my heart, there was turmoil. Thank you for replacing that turmoil with a calm confidence that you love me and assurance that you are in control.

What area in your heart or mind was at one time in disharmony, but is now at peace?

Rewards

God recognizes our work in serving him and rewards us. Make no mistake, our sins are not canceled by our good works, but only by grace through faith in Jesus. God knows our hearts, and he blesses those whose hearts are earnestly turned toward him.

> "But you, be strong and do not lose courage, for there is reward for your work." —2 Chronicles 15:7, NASB 2020

> The LORD rewards everyone for their righteousness and faithfulness. The LORD delivered you into my hands today, but I would not lay a hand on the LORD's anointed. —1 Samuel 26:23

> And without faith it is impossible to please God, because anyone who comes to him must believe that he exists and that he rewards those who earnestly seek him. —Hebrews 11:6

My prayer: Lord, I try to live rightly, not for the purpose of earning a reward, but to please you. Seeking you, pleasing you, growing closer to you, are my rewards. Thank you for these and for all of the ways that you bless me.

What have been your rewards for seeking God, serving others, trying to live an upright life, or acts of kindness?

Hope

The hope God offers is that we will be with him in eternity. We will neither be in darkness nor swallowed up by death. We will be with him. And our hope is an expectation, not merely a desire. God has proven to be trustworthy throughout history; therefore we can believe his promises.

> We wait in hope for the LORD; he is our help and our shield. In him our hearts rejoice, for we trust in his holy name. May your unfailing love be with us, LORD, even as we put our hope in you. —Psalm 33:20–22

> May the God of hope fill you with all joy and peace as you trust in him, so that you may overflow with hope by the power of the Holy Spirit. —Romans 15:13

My prayer: Lord, I love that *hope* includes trusting—in fact, *expecting*—that something will happen. Thank you for showing me that I can trust in you and that I can confidently place my hope in you.

In what do you place your hope? If that source of hope is not God, how do you know that you are not just engaging in wishful thinking?

Victorious

Not only does God give us victory over our daily struggles, he has given us a glimpse of what eternity will look like. He has told us that he has already achieved the ultimate victory, conquering sin and death, and through him, we too will overcome.

> Now this I know: The LORD gives victory to his anointed. He answers him from his heavenly sanctuary with the victorious power of his right hand. —Psalm 20:6

> But thanks be to God! He gives us the victory through our Lord Jesus Christ. —1 Corinthians 15:57

My prayer: Sovereign God, sometimes it is good to know how everything turns out. It gives me great assurance to know that you have already won the victory against sin and death. Unfathomably, my gaining the perfect future required your offering up your Son as a perfect sacrifice. And through his death and resurrection, you have won the ultimate victory for me. Death has no power over me.

All of us have experienced the thrill of victories—large and small. What victory do you like to recall?

Everlasting

The Hebrew name *El Olam* means The Everlasting God. He had no beginning, and he will exist forever. His ways, character, and promises are eternal and will never change, so we can trust him. He will be Sovereign for all time.

> Your throne was established long ago; you are from all eternity.
> —Psalm 93:2

> But from everlasting to everlasting the LORD's love is with those who fear him, and his righteousness with their children's children. —Psalm 103:17

> His dominion is an everlasting dominion that will not pass away, and his kingdom is one that will never be destroyed.
> —Daniel 7:14b

My prayer: O Lord, my God, you and everything about you are beyond my understanding, completely "other." In my life, time is constantly ticking, ticking, ticking away. That fact is not a tyranny to me because you have invited me to spend with you all of the time beyond my earthly life. While I can't comprehend your "otherness," I am assured that I will never be alone, stranded. I am so very grateful that I can trust that your Way, Truth, and Life are everlasting.

What everlasting blessing(s) are you looking forward to experiencing after you leave this earthly life?

Shalom

There is a peace that is deeper than an absence of conflict. That peace is *shalom*, and it encompasses harmony, wholeness, prosperity, tranquility, perfection, safety, and wellness. Our God is *Jehovah Shalom*, and in him we have perfect peace.

> Then Gideon built an altar there to the LORD and called it The LORD Is Peace [*Jehovah Shalom*]. To this day it still stands at Ophrah, which belongs to the Abiezrites. —Judges 6:24, ESV

> Now may the Lord of peace himself give you peace at all times and in every way. The Lord be with all of you.
> —2 Thessalonians 3:16

My prayer: Lord, until now, I have thought of *shalom* as another word for *peace* and *peace* as a lack of strife. Now I understand that *shalom* is so much more than simple peace. The dimensions of completeness, safety, wellness, as well as tranquility have now brought me into a deeper communion with you. I know that only you offer these things. I can trust in you. Your *shalom* is perfect.

Considering all of your personal reflections, which of them bring you a sense of completeness, safety, wellness, tranquility, and closeness to God?

Amen. Hallelujah!

And so, we have finished a year of reflecting on God's character, what he is like, and the ways he is involved both in the world and in our lives. The Scriptures tell how he has acted to save each one of us—indeed the whole world—from the destruction and doom of sin. *Amen* is an affirmation meaning "so be it." *Hallelujah* is a joyful shout of praise and gratitude to our great God. Hallelujah! Amen.

Index